PROJECT

MENTORING CLASSIC

MENTORING CLASSIC

USA Economy Will Collapse In 2015 Unless 1938 Minimum Wage Law Is Repealed

STATE OF USA ECONOMIC SURVIVAL BY GREAT WRITER FREDDIE L SIRMANS SR.

Government carrying the load burden of social and family provider must end, now. This republic must end this ignorant shallow minded liberal lifetime load burden placed on our government with good intentions. "The road to hell is paved with good intentions."

Sure, after the nuclear and extended family, churches, and social organizations, and as a last resort on a temporary basis government aid is a must. But, to take on permanently a burden that has been with the private sector for over 6,000 years to me is just plain economic ignorance.

Every penny the government survives on comes from the private sector and every dependent the government adds on is one less private sector tax payer, duh. Doing that means it is only a matter of time before the well dries up. That is where the USA and western civilization stands today.

Everyone standing around waiting on big government to provide for them from cradle to grave is a very, very dangerous thing in my view. The bigger government grows the smaller its provider private sector host dwindles until the whole thing collapses. That is what's fixing to happen to this P . . . . of an economy the USA have today.

USA Economy Will Collapse In 2015 Unless 1938 Minimum Wage Law Is Repealed

The only thing that can and will save the USA economy is to repeal the evil cruel 1938 socialist minimum wage law. Any wage or price control is socialist and it ties up and cripples a free market place where it can't purge out inflation, waste, moral decay, and inefficiency.

All that is necessary to save the USA is to repeal the minimum wage law and set the free market free. Then just be still, the free market will take it from there. There is nothing on earth economically wise more powerful than a true unrestricted free market place economy with unlimited competition.

With no plus or minus wage or price controls the free market place will save the USA and western civilization. However, it won't be pretty because a lot of waste, moral decay and inefficiency must be purged in the process. That is the choice the USA faces; otherwise, to stay on course and do nothing means a sure collapse and doom.

Who knows after that, it may mean all the way back to the Stone Age? A true unrestricted free market place economy with unlimited competition has never in the history of mankind failed to produce far more jobs and everything than a nation need.
SIRMANS LOG: 16 OCTOBER 2014, 1149 HOURS.

USA Economy Will Collapse In 2015 Unless 1938 Minimum Wage Law Is Repealed

WHY I THINK THE USA HAS A P . . . . (PHONY) OF AN ECONOMY

The downfall and coming doom of the USA can all be traced to the economy. Sure, we are a nation ruled by law instead of men, but, contrary to what almost everyone thinks the economy is the ultimate ruler in a free country.

Authoritarian countries can rule with an iron fist and demand people toe the party line or else. But, in free nations people have the freedom to disagree, disobey, and to a large degree do as they please. So, law or no law the real disciplinarian that truly protects and safeguards the culture, morals, and spirituals values in free nations are the economy.

We in the USA have a weak P . . . . of an economy that can't even protect itself from inflation let alone protect the nation's culture, morals or anything else. Right now, in the USA we have strong laws on the book to stop illegal immigration, crime, and every vice you can think of, yet, damn near everything is out of control. This could never happen with an economy with any teeth or bite.

All you have to do is look back before our liberal induce welfare state and nothing was out of control, which ought to tell you something. The most important thing in maintaining a civil and orderly society is the proper raising of the young, with a balance of love and discipline. In a free nation the economy must be free and untied to maintain discipline.

Economic discipline is what safeguards and protects a nation's culture, morals, and everything else. With a true free market place economy things like the boom and bust cycle and even depressions occasionally are normal. To keep life fit to live nature must have ways to get rid of waste, moral decay, and inefficiency.

Otherwise, there can be no rebirth or re-growth. Then it may be all the way back to the Stone Age the way we are headed. It is even possible for man to disappear from the globe. I could go on and on, on how important a true free market place economy is to the survival of any free nation, but I will start closing this down.

We must untie and free our economy from what the shallow minded liberals did to it by enacting this evil 1938 socialist minimum wage law. What that evil law did was take the strength and power to fight off inflation away from the USA economy. And even today the USA economy doesn't have the power or strength to fight off inflation, let alone protect the nation's culture and morals.

The economy the USA has today is an almost

useless, weak, p . . . . of an economy, not a strong kick-ass disciplinarian job producing machine that produced the roaring twenties. Only repealing the evil 1938 socialist minimum wage law can save this great nation. I can only pray that wise men/women will do their duty to save our beloved country.

My extremely wise supernatural wisdom is as threatening to the republican establishment as it is to the liberals and Dem's in my view. You can love me or hate me, but my only concern is the survival of my country. And I'm one that still truly believes in duty, honor, country above all else.

SIRMANS LOG: 02 OCTOBER 2014, 1543 HOURS

LIBERALS THINK RICH PEOPLE ARE STUPID!!!
scroll down

GREAT WRITER FREDDIE L SIRMANS SR GIVES THE ROCK-HARD COLD-STEEL TRUTH ON DOMESTIC ABUSE
All I hear is abuse, abuse, wife abuse, child abuse, women abuse and on and on to no end. Liberal women are almost up in arms; and if it was left up to them they would de-nut all men and make sissies out of all of us. To me there is no mystery here, men are just being men, and it is just cause and effect in

action in my view. Men are aggressive creatures by nature and are only doing what they are allowed to get away with. And it is a pipe dream to expect law enforcement to do more than put a dent in it.

It takes fighting fire with fire to really stamp out or completely get under control domestic type violence of this sort. It takes a lot of loved ones that are willing to make a personal sacrifice to truly stamp out or control domestic violence. There has always been some domestic abuse but never out of control like what we are seeing today.

What we are seeing today is the result of a lack of the strong nuclear and extended family unit. Today we have too few no-none-sense kick-ass dads or brothers that are prepared to go to hell or prison before they will tolerate this sort of abuse on a love one. We are too busy using the "N" word on each other to give a damn. Very few cousins or good friends are prepared to make such a sacrifice.

I have personally heard a few men say that the only thing keeping me off her ass is her dad would kill me. Sure, law enforcement will do their job and enforce the law, but no law enforcement agency can protect private citizens 24-7 day in and day out. Even if women are the weaker sex old man colt solved that imbalance many, many years ago by creating an equalizer. But, the thing about that is not all of us have the will or the guts to send a S.O.B. to hell.

SIRMANS LOG: 19 SEPTEMBER 2014, 2216 HOURS

It really is a waste of time trying to get a liberal to understand freedom and a free market place. That is why most of the world is poor and will always be poor. The point I'm making is liberals don't really understand freedom. Freedom means every individual has a free choice. Jobs don't just drop out of heaven, someone just like you and I must create or provide a job.

This is the land of the free and no one puts a gun to anyone's head and forces them to work for minimum wages. Everyone in this great country has the right to create his/her own job or quit any job one doesn't like. Most liberals think it is wrong for some people to enjoy the rich life while most stay poor. Right now if the liberals had the power they would take almost everything from the rich and spend it on social programs.

They are too shallow minded to realize that rich people are not stupid. They really believe rich people would continue producing and providing jobs while almost all of their earnings are being taken away. I just can't understand how anyone with any common sense could be so shallow, but they are, and are running the country, too.

There never has and never will be a rich and wealthy nation without a lot of rich greedy people to make it happen. If left entirely up to the liberals the USA would in no time be a third world nation. Yet, enough wanting something for nothing voters keep the tax and spend liberals in power while the country goes to hell in a hand basket.

SIRMANS LOG: 12 JANUARY 2014, 2341 HOURS

A HALF OF A LOAF IS BETTER THAN NOTHING!

IF YOU THINK IT'S GETTING BAD NOW WITH OBAMACARE, YOU HAVEN'T SEEN NOTHING YET, YOU JUST WAIT, IF THE DEM'S WIN ANYTHING IN NOV. 2014, THEN WE WILL GET THE FULL THROBBING PURPLE SHAFT FROM THE DEMOCRATS. THEY WANT TO FIRST SECURE THE 2014 MIDTERM ELECTION BEFORE THEY RAM THE FULL SHAFT TO US. IT WILL BE EVEN LESS JOBS AND A TRILLION MORE IN DEBT. IT WILL BE LIKE DETROIT CITY NATIONWIDE! THINK ABOUT IT, WE WILL THEN GET ALL OF OBAMACARE, AND DRY, TOO. GOD, I ASK IN YOUR NAME SAVE THIS GREAT NATION.

USA Economy Will Collapse In 2015 Unless 1938 Minimum Wage Law Is Repealed

It doesn't bother me a lot when I don't sell a lot of books. That is because I estimate only around 2 percent of the American population has the depth and wisdom to truly understand what the hell I be talking about. So be it, I carry on.

They can't get pass the fact that it is not the amount of money that truly matters; it is the buying power that really counts. Before the New deal which started the welfare state $5.00 would buy more than $50.00 will today.

Repealing the minimum wage law would put the provider role back into the hands of the people and allow this great country to survive. Otherwise, there is no way in hell the USA is going to survive on its present course.

Just keep on believing in this phony minimum wage economy and without a doubt within a year I will be proven right. We'll soon see just how nutty my predictions are.

The repeal of the minimum wage law is our savior, but, 98 percent of the population can't get pass believing more and bigger is always better. But, to me a half of a loaf is better than nothing because nothing is what this nation is going to get if we don't change course.

SIRMANS LOG: 29 DECEMBER 2013, 1022 HOURS

MAN/WOMAN OVERBOARD, USA ECONOMY SHIP IS BEGINNING TO SINK!
Folks, I'm just a lowly unknown writer out here pounding away trying to get through to thick sculls. Very few actually know about me or my books, and most of those that do are not interesting in tough accountability and responsibility. But, I know without a doubt at some point my writing will be vindicated.

Reality is reality there is just no way of getting around that fact. Sure, sometimes it takes a while for the results to catch up but there are no free rides in life someone always pays. The liberals and Dem's have been very successful; they have created masses upon masses of government dependents. They have convinced these dependents that government will always be there to take care of them and their needs.

That is not reality that is the biggest lie that has ever been told. There has never been a government that didn't go broke at some point. The free market place made the USA the most richest and powerful nation to ever exist. The government didn't do that, the free market place did that. Now, I believe most of the people running our government today doesn't even believe in a free market place.

I believe most of the people in charge of our government today are socialist or communist at heart. Everyone seems to be so surprised about how the liberals and Dem's connived and forced Obamacare down our throats. There is nothing new here about liberals in my view. How in the hell do you think the liberals and Dem's held on to the USA house of Representative for 40 consecutive years.

They did it by lying and conniving, and that is what is really happening with this Obamacare website. They will never let it work right before the November 2014 election. They intend to keep the confusion going and never let all of the high costs be widely known before the 2014 election. But, God help us If the Dem's win anything in November 2014, because if they do they are going to ram the full purple shaft to this free nation, e.g. Obamacare dry like it or not.

I believe these people are hardcore ideologues and will go down with the ship before yielding an inch, and believe me that is exactly what is about to happen. Trust me, this USA economy ship is taking on too big of a load and is beginning to sink. This ship is going down unless most of its government load is jettisoned, and fast.

However, the only way to lighten governments load is to kick it out of its social and family provider role. And the way to do that is repeal the minimum wage law or else, this economy ship is going down. I suspect many of the rats have already left the ship in spirit and have property in in places like New Zealand and Australia.

SIRMANS LOG: 26 DECEMBER 2013, 1840 HOURS

WHO IS THE AFRICAN AMERICAN COMMUNITY'S DADDY?
I'm fixing to briefly weigh in on something I

have no business touching, besides, some people think of me as a nut case anyway. What if I am off the beaten path that don't mean my beliefs are wrong. Even a broken clock is right twice a day. Concerning two great black athletes that is at loggerheads: Long before O. J. got into trouble, guess who was always on his case for being too white? Go figure? Some people just naturally goes against the grain, enough said. The problem with the African American race as a whole is culture.

The welfare state has destroyed the African American family structure and community. But, that don't mean we have to take it lying down and still not feel responsible for our own behavior and survival. I don't have the power to stop anything, but you can bet your bottom dollar that I will never make excuses for bad behavior. And no matter who does it I'm not accepting any excuses because of what happened in the distance past.

Grow up African Americans and take responsibility for the behavior of yourself and that of your race. This welfare state has destroyed accountability and responsibility throughout all of America and I'm sick and tired of it. Today a decent law abiding black man can't walk into many stores without being feared because we as a race won't clean up our own community house.

USA Economy Will Collapse In 2015 Unless 1938 Minimum Wage Law Is Repealed

Don't tell me that ain't from a lack of feeling responsible for our own behavior as individuals and as a race. We still have a dependent slave mentality and think it's the white mans fault. The only cure for that is for someone to kick the crutch from under us and demand we stand on our own two feet. Independent minded people don't look to blame and find excuses to fail. I know I may sounds cold, but this USA economy is fixing to collapse and we black folks need to wake up and be prepared, now.

Every preacher in the pulpit and any member in the black community with an ounce of authority need to feel responsible for this cancer in our community called crime. I don't mean taking any physical action we have law enforcement for that. What I'm talking about is taking a moral stand instead of not feeling racially responsible for bad behavior in our youth.

If we don't save our youths no other race will. I didn't intend to vent like this, I just got carried away but something's need to be said. The so called African American leadership is out to lunch.
SIRMANS LOG: 18 DECEMBER 2013, 1750 HOURS

THERE IS NO GOVERNMENT SYSTEM EVER TO EXIST MORE SELF-

DESTRUCTIVE THAN A WELFARE STATE!

Like a junkie on the streets trying to get a fix there is nothing a welfare state won't sell off to support its seized social and family provider role. As long as the USA government stays in its social and family provider role it will be impossible for the USA to stop reckless spending or survive.

Right now, the liberals doesn't have the survival instinct or the wisdom to see a real need to stop spending. They are living in the moment and can't see any real danger in reckless spending, and you couple that with an economically ignorant main stream press and general public, all I know to do is pray.

Abolishing the minimum wage law will give the social and family provider role back to the people where it belongs and has always been until the "New deal" seized it in 1938. God I ask in your name, "Save the USA." Time is a winding down, I don't know how much we have left, but, I know beyond a shadow of doubt that a total economic collapse is near unless drastic changes are made.

When I look at the future I think the republicans will soon get the power to have their shot at this health care thing. But, I have news for them too, just like the Dem's they think government can keep and hold on to its social and family provider role, wrong.

USA Economy Will Collapse In 2015 Unless 1938 Minimum Wage Law Is Repealed

I believe unless the republicans and conservatives set about abolishing the minimum wage law they will be seen as phony liberals and quickly replaced. But, of course do like the Dem's never admit in advance what your real intentions are, just git in there and rid the country of this Minimum wage law. It's a free market place killer. See Sirmans survival plan further down.

Most of the big cities water, sewage, and bridges infrastructure were built before a minimum wage law, so, don't tell me junking the minimum wage law won't save this great nation. And here is the real kicker: The USA economy is still the economic engine of the world and if it collapses it takes the world economy down with it. Sure, the world economy may bail us, but not before owning us.

The apple cart has been upset and the only thing that can save the USA is a true free market place. Pure communism and socialism never has and never will work, but, now we have a new monster far worse than both of those systems to contend with, it's called the welfare state. There is no system ever to exist more self-destructive than a welfare state.

It leaves almost no survival tools in place to survival on when nature's bust cycle comes around or if the economy collapses. It really is no joke when I say it may be all the way back to the Stone age for modern civilization. We have no strong nuclear and extended family system to survive on. We have centralized factory farming for our meats and vegetables and hardly any small farmers and home gardeners.

That means we have no adequate emergency backup bartering capacity if the economy collapses and money is worthless. And on and on, our family morals and values would make dog eat dog look like a Sunday picnic after a week into a collapse. Wages and prices must be free floating for a genuine free market place to work and that can't happen with a minimum wage law or any kind of wage or price control.

The consumer cost of living is what's going to kill off the USA economy and Obamacare just speeds up the process. Here is the Ultimatum: Either the USA government abolish the minimum wage law which will free the people to save themselves and the country, or it tries to consolidate and hold on to its current social and family provider role.

If it chooses the latter there is no doubt in my mind that it will to no avail sell off the country to foreigners to try to hang on to a role it shouldn't be in, in the first place. You just watch, and the wait won't be very long. I

can dissect an economy as well as anyone
and that is what I predict is going to happen.
You can't get blood out of a turnip.

I doubt there is any gold left at Fort Knox and
there is no telling what else has already been
sold off by the federal reserve. I'm telling you
as a man of great super natural wisdom,
unless the minimum wage law is abolished
we might as well kiss our freedom and this
great country good by forever.

**SIRMANS LOG: 04 DECEMBER 2013,
2217 HOURS**

**AMERICA! YOU HAVE BEEN SOLD A
FALSE BILL OF GOODS**

There is a sucker born everyday. It amazes
me how gullible people are. They have fallen
for this cock & bull big lie that the Obamacare
website is somehow a big screw-up, wrong. I
for one don't buy that for one second. A
computer or a website must obey what it is
programmed to do.

The problem is: There is no way in the hell
liberals and Dem's are going to let it be
known on a large scale the double and triple
cost the people will face until after November
2014. Get a grip America; you have been
sold a false bill of goods. And be prepared for
a never ending list of excuses, but, you will
never get a proper working website with cost
no matter what you are told. I rest my case.

**SIRMANS LOG: 30 NOVEMBER 2013,
2216 HOURS**

**THE ROOT CAUSE FOR USA AND
WESTERN CIVILIZATION AVOIDABLE
COMING DOOM
NEW ADD ON: 17 SEPT. 2014, 1004
HOURS,** scroll down

One thing that gives me an advantage over
most people is the ability to penetrate
through fog and bore to the core of an issue.
A lot of people think some kind of tax fix is
the answer to the nation's problems. And
there are others that think some kind of
convention of the states is the answer.

But, I'm here to tell you nothing is going to
save the USA and western civilization unless
the core root problem is dealt with. And
through all of the fog and side Issues I see it
all alone standing there the core and root
problem itself. The core and root cause for
the coming doom and destruction of the USA
and western civilization is: "Government in
the role of social and family provider."

Now government is personally responsible for
millions upon millions of mouths to feed. And
with its power to tax and spend nothing is
going to stop it from caring for it's
dependents in that role, period. Never in
6,000 years of written history on a mass
scale has a government taken on such a

permanent burden before the "New deal"
came along.

Even in socialist and communist countries
there are make work jobs. And until the USA
government surrenders the provider role back
to the private sector nuclear and extended
family system this nation cannot and will not
be saved from total doom. However, the big
problem is acquiring the vehicle to get us
back to depending on the bread and butter
nuclear family system before our USA
government crashes and burns.

The only vehicle on earth with the power to
get the USA back on track is the all mighty all
powerful free market place. However, with
the USA there is problem, the USA has a P . .
. . of an economy.

No problem that can be fixed, the USA
economy is just hog tied and has no power to
discipline itself due to the evil 1938 socialist
minimum wage law. And that can easily be
remedies by repealing the evil 1938 socialist
minimum wage law, then a free untied all
powerful free market place economy will take
it from there and save this great nation.

Even on an individual basis a head of
household provider is going to do everything
within his/her power to feed and care for
his/her dependents. There have been many
cases where a family provider would beg,

borrow, and steal to feed its dependents. So, it only stands to reason with government's power to tax and spend nothing is going to stop it from taxing production and producers to death to feed its dependents.

The only way to deal with government as a family provider is to get it out of that role, period.

ADD ON: 17 SEPTEMBER 2014, 1004 HOURS

The private sector nuclear and extended family system is the only thing that can carry the social and family provider load over the long haul, period. Through shallow minded ignorance the liberals put this load and burden on a permanent basis on the USA government and it has been there ever since the "New deal."

Now, it has simply become too heavy for the USA government to carry it any longer, which is going to make it impossible for the USA economy to survive. There is simply no doubt in my mind the USA economy is going to soon crash, and our only hope is to repeal the evil 1938 socialist minimum wage law before it is too late.

If that is done in time that will transfer the load and burden back where it has always been for over 6,000 years with the private

sector. And that will free up government to collect taxes, protect the interior, fight wars, etc.. That is the only thing that is going to save our USA P . . . . of an economy from a total collapse and soon.
We have no other choice if the great USA is to survive, period.
SIRMANS LOG: 16 SEPTEMBER 2016, 1348 HOURS

RAY RICE EPISODE, SEPT. 14, 2014 ADD ON, SCROLL DOWN
As a rule I stay away from commenting on hot button emotional issues, but to me it seems to be something sinister going on with this Ray Rice case and I decided to weigh in. Like it says in the good book let who is without sin throw the first stone seems to be totally forgotten.

No decent self-respecting human being is going to condone a vastly more powerful man knocking a woman out for any reason, period. However, we all are human and to err in itself is human.

If provoked enough we all have a snapping point, then you couple that with possibly two intoxicated individuals, who is to say who is victimized, here, reality is reality. Sure, punishment is due, but to take a man's lively hood away and totally destroy him for bad judgment and possibly too much to drink is overkill in my view.

People tend to live on a standard equal to their income and he probably owes a lot of people a lot of money. It is hard enough now for a woman to get a man to make a commitment, and crucifying punishment like this means passive type women are in and aggressive independent type women are out, reality is reality.

What concerns me about the whole thing is this liberal created political correctness hog wash. If this political correctness nonsense continues we will end up with a P . . . . of a nation just like we already have a P . . . . of an economy.

I will stop here, I have already said too much, I hope I don't end up begging on the streets due to the political correctness mob like what they may do to Ray Rice.

These shallow minded liberals don't understand profit, individual freedom, or anything, they think survival is a pie train, almost everything in this great nation is upside down, God help us.

ADD ON: SEPT. 14, 2014
All of this ado and emotional hype about this case is not from football fans and the general public in my view. I think it is extreme

liberalism gone amok. I see this as an individual case that has been turned into a mountain out of a mole hill. But, extreme liberalism want to turn it into some kind of domestic violence movement.

Culture-wise we are past the point of no return when one can't spank or discipline one's child anymore, that in itself is a threat to law enforcement everywhere, but liberals are too shallow to see that.

When undisciplined youngster that have never been conditioned to act with restraint when dealing with frustration reach adulthood only law enforcement stands between them and an orderly safe environment.

A child's basic personality is shaped by the age of six and many a first grade school teachers can point out even at that age the ones that will most likely end up in prison. That is our welfare state and liberalism in action.

Spare the rod you spoil the child is as valid today as it was 2000 years ago. Liberalism has destroyed this great nation and I'm just one lone neurotic mentally handicapped cripple trying to make a stand.

I don't expect most people to agree with me, but think God we live in a country where I won't disappear in the middle of the night.

Praise be to God.
**SIRMANS LOG: 12 SEPTEMBER 2014,
1559 HOURS**

CONSERVATISM VERSUS COLD REALITY
I consider myself to be conservative, but
even more so a realist. In terms of gaining
and keeping power I think the establishment
republican party is taking the right course.

However, I also think the conservatives and
tea party is right on what is best for the long
term survival of our nation, but their policies
will guarantee that the Dems stay in power
and they never get power. The Dems created
our welfare state and with them in power the
good old USA will never get control of suicide
spending.

With the establishment republicans in power
the suicide spending train to hell will be
slowed down considerately but not enough to
avoid eventually reaching doom. My heart
and soul is with the conservatives and tea
party because they know this country's
survival is at stake, but they are eighty years
too late to make a do or die stand.

Conservatives allowed the liberals to enact
two "New deal" programs that this great
nation will never recovery from unless they
are eliminated and soon. The first program
was government seizing and taking on the

role of social and family provider. That means government starts feeding on itself and taxing production until there is nothing left to tax. Duh?

The second program was enacting the cruel evil 1938 socialist minimum wage law. The cruel and evilness of this law means the death of a true free market economy, that is why I drumbeat so hard on ridding this nation of this monster.

This law alone is what allowed the shallow brained liberals to cripple the USA economy to the point it don't have the power to fight off inflation, which lead to the destruction of our culture, morals, and values. A true free market economy without a choking minimum wage law would never allow hoards of foreign invaders to flood into this great country.

That is because the demand wouldn't be there. Those now on welfare would have all of those jobs the invaders are seeking. And there wouldn't be any welfare for anyone to free load on, an unshackled free USA economy would never tolerate it. Sure, we have a welfare state today but I guarantee you we won't have one very much longer. Yet, we march on deeper into fantasy land.

Otherwise, the strong nuclear and extended family system, churches, and social organizations would be strong enough to meet social needs like through out history. And temporary government help would only be a last resort. Now, when this welfare state soon totally collapses the USA and western civilization may fall all the way back to the Stone Age. Wake up America, I'm for real, this is no joking matter.

The liberals from both political parties created this entitlement gimmy, gimmy populace as huge as ninety percent to some degree. So, lets face it, most of these masses of government dependents will never bite the hand that feeds them.

Sure, in some cases hardcore conservatives and tea party members are going to get elected, but to become a majority party in power ain't going to happen. I will sum it up by saying anyone that have read my work know I offer a solution. And I know it will take a miracle for my solution to happen.

I don't know how the almighty is going to make it happen but I believe some way some how it will happen, it must. The evil 1938 socialist minimum wage law must be repealed it is the only solution.

Repealing the minimum wage law will set free the might USA economy that is still shackled and tired up from the evil 1938 socialist minimum wage law. No other force on this earth has the power to save the USA from

USA Economy Will Collapse In 2015 Unless 1938 Minimum Wage Law Is Repealed

total doom.

A free genuine true free market place economy has never failed to save a dying nation. Don't doubt me; my destiny is to keep sounding the distress call for survival.

Unlike authoritarian type governments, free countries with private property rights must rely on the free market place to maintain discipline and protect its culture, morals, and values. That is because people have the right to be stupid or anyway they want to be.

Right now 95 percent of the American people believe a higher minimum wage and making more money will solve their problems. That is like treating ones big toe thinking it will solve a heart problem.

The fact is its not how much money one makes that matters, it is far more important how much can be bought with the money one does make. The path we are on is fast destroying what little buying power our money has left. It actually happened in Germany where it took a wheel barrow load of money to buy a loaf of bread.

There is no mystery on what ails the USA economy, the answer is very simple, the USA economy is totally out of balance, period. All that is necessary to set the USA economy back in balance is to set it free.

We set it free minus the choking and crippling 1938 minimum wage law, and then the economy will balance and fix itself. That is if government just stays the hell out of the free market place, and stay with collecting taxes.

Don't doubt me, there is no other way to save the USA no matter what the learned economist and egg heads tell you. Nothing in nature can exist without completing some form of rebirth cycle, and the USA is long over due.

SIRMANS LOG: 28 AUGUST 2014, 2246 HOURS

WHY MOST AFRICAN AMERICANS WILL NEVER VOTE REPUBLICAN?

African Americans are bonded to the Democrat party like a mother and child. And any Republican that thank he can break that bond is fooling himself. It is an exercise in futility; it can't be done by an outsider.

I'm no scholar on the subject, but I am a great thinker with super natural wisdom. I see mother and child like bonding as a phenomenon in nature. Super strong bonding doesn't just happen by accident there is a caretaking survival element involved.

Sure, when born a mother may love her baby because it is hers but the super strong bonding builds from day to day caring for it. In fact a stray animal, plant, or anything that one feeds and provide water will bring about a bond and deep caring for it.

Two equals tend not to bond. Two dependents tend not to bond. The strongest bonding tends to occur when there is a provider and a dependent. An unselfish provider will always try to wean a dependent to become independent and stand on his own.

The mother eagle provider break the bond by kicking her young out of the nest thereby forcing them to provide for themselves. African Americans are mentally in the nest of the democrat party and that is where we will stay as along as the welfare state keeps the masses of social programs going.

As to the republicans, never mind the nation being bankrupted, you are the enemy for being too stingy. However, there is a real problem for the Dems, this thing called "Reality" keep trying to raise its ugly head. The reality is the USA is dead broke and can't continue footing the bill for mass provider and social spending.

The liberals are already gutting the military like Western Europe has already done to free up funds. I keep providing the solution but no one wants to hear it because it doesn't fit our mass economic ignorant thinking.

I will repeat it for the umpteenth time, repeal
the evil 1938 socialist minimum wage law,
now, that will set the USA economy free and
it will save us all. Through out history a true
genuine free market place has never failed to
save a nation by producing jobs and more
than enough of everything a nation needs.

Otherwise, we go down, we are all doomed
when this great nation's economy soon
collapses. Don't doubt me; I can dissect an
economy as well as anyone.
**SIRMANS LOG: 26 AUGUST 2014, 1639
HOURS**

How I grow my container garden.
I decided to share my container garden with
you because I believe the USA in a very few
years is going to face mass starvation.
I'm going to make it short and not go into
any long details.

Container gardening is the fastest growing
form of gardening there is today. It is so
simple almost anybody can do it. In most
cases even people in the cities can do it. All
one needs is some containers and potted soil.

You can grow almost anything in a container

that you can grow in the ground. The biggest problem is limited space, especially when it comes to vines and running plants.

Myself, I don't like to do a lot of bending over so I bought some wide cement blocks and some 2"x10"x8' pressure treated boards to sit my pots on.

In most cases at least a 5 gallon container should be used. You don't have to use expensive flower pots; just any 5 gallon bucket will do as long as drain holes are put on the side at the bottom. Potted soil ranges from the cheap to the expensive.

Myself, I use the cheapest and get very good results. For planting: Seeds will come up after about 2 ½ days when planted about ½ inch deep and watered daily. However, I prefer to just buy the plants and everything I need from a garden center in Wal-mart, Lowe's, Home depot, or any plant store or nursery.

Once the planting is done I add water per plant each day or as needed. I make sure there is adequate drain off to prevent root rot, just place a saucer like holder you can buy at the store under each pot.

Lastly, to get good growth and high yield I
add about 1/2 gallon of liquid
Miracle Gro fertilizer per plant every 2 weeks
or so, just follow directions on box. There are
2 types of tomatoes indeterminate and
determinate.

The determinate type limits the size to 3 or 4
feet, which is best because of limited space.
Also it is always best to limit it to 1 plant per
pot to get the best yield.

The number of container plants I have this
season is: 4 Tomatoes, 3 Bell peppers, 2
Banana peppers, 5 Okra, 2 Collard greens, 2
Turnip greens, and 2 Mustard greens.

Also, I keep on hand a bottle of vegetable
insect spray to zap any intruders I see, but
make sure the kind you use can be used up
to the day of harvesting.

I have enjoyed sharing my container garden
with you, hopeful you will try one for
yourself, go for it.

Anyone can do it all it takes is to just try, all

it takes is just a few feet of space as long as
the sun can get to your plant. Good luck on
your fresh home grown tomatoes. Make sure
the plants are placed where the sun can get
to them, they do make growing lamps but
that is a different story that I know little
about.

MAN HAS NEVER SET FOOT ON THE MOON? SIRMANS LOG: 02 JUNE 2013, 1750 HOURS

Awhile back I wrote an article that I was 99.9
percent sure that man landed on the moon
but I still can't get past that .1 percent. It's
not that I am dumb or stupid; I understand
electronics and modern science.

Right out of high school back in 1962 I took a
six month course in radio and TV repair. Back
then we studied mainly the super heterodyne
receiver and vacuum tubes. The transistor
was just coming into play the same as the
cathode ray vacuum tube which was the early
TV.

We also learned about waves and
frequencies. So, on my part it just doesn't
make any sense for me to doubt that they

landed on the moon. When I wrote the first article on this subject a guy asked me in a comment did I have any proof that they didn't land on the moon, and I said "No."

In replying I told him it was just a gut feeling, and that is still what haunts me on how I feel about the whole matter. There is something about this whole thing that logical just doesn't add up in my way of thinking. I feel something is wrong somewhere.

Even if they did land, maybe they found something up there (UFO) that they are not telling. I have a fair understanding of human nature, and there have never been a case where man opened up a new frontier and didn't exploit it in some way.

Like I said, maybe there is a big hidden mystery that maybe it's better the public never knows about. I don't have any inside information, just a raw gut feeling. This article may be the smoking gun or the last straw that I really am a nut, kook, or loon, who cares, some already believe that anyway.

However, I am not entirely alone doubting

that man landed on the moon, 10 percent of the USA population is Doubting Thomas's on this. God bless America.

PS: I see where they use the terrain in the state of Utah to train for the moon landing. You don't suppose they use that same terrain to make moon landing movies do you? (Just kidding y'all).

THE USA LAST SUPPER!
SIRMANS LOG: 9 JUNE 2013, 1954 HOURS
Anyone that can stomach reading my work knows that I have a super mind agree or not. So, I have decided to draw a picture and explain what happened to the great USA. I think it boils down to two word "Sound judgment."

Starting with me, probably three percent or less of the USA population agree or truly understand my way of thinking. The vast majority think my writing is some kind of nineteenth century throwback. And they are mostly right, a hundred years ago about ninety five percent of the USA population would have agreed with my way of thinking.

USA Economy Will Collapse In 2015 Unless 1938 Minimum Wage Law Is Repealed

Back then same sex marriage and mass killing in the womb would have been beyond everyone's imagination. Now, ninety five percent or more of the USA population see that as normal. The USA is about evenly split down the middle in terms of voting.

The masses of government dependents see the republicans as the enemy and believe they would like to take away their livelihood. The other half believes the democrats are going to tax and spend the USA out of existence. But, I believe like one politician said: "There is not a dime worth of difference between the two parties."

Sure, there are minor differences in terms of appointing judges but neither party is going to serious stop the growth of government. Overall the Dems and liberals are the reason the USA is in the dire situation it is today. In my view Dems and liberals are just plain shallow, but, super aggressive and will not let morality, country, or anything stand in the way of them grabbing and taking power.

On the other hand the Republican Party has become almost as liberal as the democrat party. I feel the conservatives ought to just flat out take it over. Even conservatives don't agree with my out dated thinking, still I think they are the only ones that can save the USA from total doom.

The thing is they don't know how. Well, it may already be too late but I am going to tell them how to save the USA. However, I'm sure they won't agree and won't take my advice; still I'm going to pass it on anyway. Remember, I said the Key words were "Sound judgment." The Dems and liberals own the thinking and shaping of young minds in the USA.

For over 6,000 years up until the "New deal" the nuclear and extended family system was the primary shaper of young minds, but, not anymore. To a great extent in most situations now the primary shaper of young minds is liberal TV and the liberal school systems. Very few homes are instilling traditional conservative's norms and values.

Almost everything the young comes in contact with now-a-days is liberal. So, of course the young when they mature will not have a conservative foundation to return to like children of old. "Sound judgment" which is everything to keep and maintain a civil society will soon be nowhere to be found.

So, my advice to conservatives is follow my advice cold turkey and go for the jugular. No if ands or buts, fight to abolish the minimum wage law now, not tomorrow. With no minimum wage law the government will lose it power to control private property.

With no minimum wage law government would have to give up its provider role which has all but destroyed our nuclear and extended family system. With no minimum wage law manufacturing would return to the USA and everything would be made in America with jobs for all.

With no minimum wage law the economy would balance itself and the poor could pay their own food and medical bills. With no minimum wage law people would make far less money but $5.00 would buy A week's worth of grocery. And I could go on and on what has been proven to work for over 6,000 years before the "New deal."

Plus here are the cold steel facts, if the

USA Economy Will Collapse In 2015 Unless 1938 Minimum Wage Law Is Repealed

minimum wage law is not abolished, the USA is not going to survive and that is a guarantee. Before the "New deal" the male nuclear family provider hands on instilled and enforced norms and traditional conservatives values thereby safe guarding our human survival.

Now, unless the government is kicked out of the provider role the USA has the chance of a snowball in hell of surviving. Abolishing the minimum wage will get the ball rolling on saving my beloved homeland.

I believe in a few months when Obamacare fully kicks in it is going to explode the dole and cause the USA economy to crash and burn. I also believe abolishing the minimum wage law is the only way to stop the USA economy from crashing and burning.

Will congress abolish the minimum wage law? NO! Will the USA and western civilization survive? NO! Reason, the boom and bust cycle is a part of nature the same as the life and death cycle.

Abolishing the minimum wage law would have save us by allowing the bust cycle to complete it normal rotation, but no, the learned economist and egg heads think they can juggle the figures forever, wrong.

Call me a fool or nut as you wish, but without a doubt I know I am right on this. Sure, no one agrees with me on any of this but they will, the hardship and suffering just hasn't taken it toll yet.

USA SUPREME COURT CONFIRMS THE VALIDITY OF MY WRITING!

For over twenty years even I at times have questioned the worth or validity of my writing. But, not anymore, since the supreme court all but struck down the defensive marriage act on 26 JUNE 2013.

Folks, it's over for the great USA and western civilization. And the really sad part is very few people even realize it. It is very simple, there has never been and never will be a civilization that last over 80-100 years without a strong nuclear and extended family system, period.

What the Supreme Court did was drive the final nail in the coffin of a strong nuclear and extended family system. Now! Let me tell you why I know I am right beyond a shadow of a doubt. The nuclear and extended family

system has kept civilization intact for over
6,000 years.

That was until the early 1930's in the USA
when a group of liberal geniuses did
something that had never been done in the
history of mankind; they seized the family
provider role for the government itself. Wow!
Wham! Bam! Armed with the "New deal"
programs the government became "The great
white father" and sugar daddy.

What the shallow minded liberals failed to
realize and still haven't to this day is
understand that the provider role is the Key
to civilization and its survival. What is taught
and instilled in the young is what maintains
and keep society stable and intact.

Norms and traditions must be instilled for
safety and survival because they are based
on past trial and experience. This must duty
for over 6,000 years was tasked to the
provider of each nuclear family unit. The
nuclear family provider is the only one with
the power and authority to make sure this
must duty is carried out.

The family provider should have the physical,
financial, and moral capacity to perform this
duty thereby safeguarding and maintaining a
healthy civilized society. Well, we all know
what happened; the USA government seized
the provider role for itself and got drunk on

power. So, you can forget about it yielding
even one inch, ever.

Sure, it provided food and shelter, but failed
to enforce any other must provider duty.
Failure by the government as the provider to
make sure norms and traditions were instilled
in the young meant death to the USA four
generations into the future. And sure enough
here we are around four generations later
with almost everything ass backward.

Same sex marriage and mass killing in the
womb seem to be the norm today which
would have been insane at the time, and now
sound judgment is something you find in the
history books. And, you are going to convince
me that this nation can survive,
@#%$*%$#, I love you too!

But, due to my great supernatural wisdom I
see one last chance for the USA to survive.
And we can still survive with freedom still
intact provided we as a nation abolish the
minimum wage law; otherwise we go the way
of the great Auk.
**SIRMANS LOG: 27 JUNE 2013, 1255
HOURS**

**THE FULL DESTRUCTIVE FORCE OF
OBAMACARE IS FIXING TO HIT!**
All seems to be calm and quiet on the home
front; they say the housing market is

booming. So, what is there to fear? It is almost always quiet before the storm. I'll tell you what's lurking out there, the full destructive force of Obamacare is about to hit.

I also predict that the dole is likely to explode and then all hell is going to break lose when Obamacare fully hit. So, my advice is brace yourself the s... is about to hit the fan. There is already a mad rush by businesses to stay below 50 employees and keep the work week below 30 hours.

There is already over 48,000.000 million on the food stamps dole alone, plus, we are already $17,000.000.000.000 trillion in debt and borrowing 40 cents of every dollar the government spends. Now, you are going to convince me otherwise that at some point the USA government is not going to prostitute our sovereignty away?#@%!, spare me.

So, in a few more months when Obamacare fully kicks in it may be Katie bar the door. In my view everything Washington enacts now if it's not to abolish the minimum wage law is going to be an exercise in futility.

I think the USA is at a do or die stage, and dealing with the root problem first is a must and anything else is a waste of precious time. I see the USA destructive root problem as government's seized role of being a "Social and family provider."

The USA government as a social and family provider has ran it course which is a role it should never have gotten into in the first place. The "New deal" seized the provider role from the nuclear and extended family system where it had been for over 6,000 years.

Until the USA government gets the hell out of the social and family provider business the USA cannot and will not survive, period. It's just that simple, either the USA government jettisons its social and family provider role or we go the way of the great auk, there is no way to get around that fact.

The only way to save the USA before a total economic collapse results from Obamacare and an exploding dole is to abolish the minimum wage law now. I know in today's climate very few has the wisdom or depth to see how abolishing the minimum wage would save the USA economy.

That is why I really don't see the minimum wage ever being abolishing voluntarily, still, I must never stop pounding for it. Even if no one else do I know only abolishing the minimum wage can safely bleed off the pressure and save the USA economy, because there is no doubt in my mind it is fixing to blow or collapse.

USA Economy Will Collapse In 2015 Unless 1938 Minimum Wage Law Is Repealed

Sure, before the "New deal" there was much suffering especially the elderly. But, the tried and true nuclear and extended family provider system has proven itself for over 6,000 years, it's not perfect, but it works and doesn't destroy morality. Plus, the nuclear and extended family provider system is never a threat to bring down the whole system and send us all back to the Stone Age.

Whereas, the "New deal" has given us this tax hungry welfare state socialist beast. This beast has all but destroyed the nuclear family, family values, and sunk our morals to the point that we have same sex marriage and mass killing of the unborn in the womb. And even worse, very few USA citizens even care or give a damn, to them that's just the new norm.

Yet, someone like me is seen as a nut case and a throw back that should be ignored or locked away some where. With all of this going on the USA cannot and will not survive unless the minimum wage is abolished to bring back some sanity.

We are just too far gone into this swamp of value rot and moral decay, only a physical barrier like abolishing the minimum wage can save us now. Man is control by logic and self-interest which means the way to hell is paved with good intentions.

"Be still God will fight your battle," but, in
this case, abolish the "Minimum wage law,
then be still, and the invisible hand which is
nature's supreme law of "Natural selection"
will save the USA economy and western
civilization, too.
**SIRMANS LOG: 9 MAY 2013, 1243
HOURS.**

**FREDDIE L SIRMANS SR. SHORT BASIC
LECTURE ON UNDERSTANDING AN
ECONOMY!**
Am I dumb, ignorant, or just plain stupid, I'm
sure many people think so because I keep
harping on abolishing the minimum wage
law. What if I am a kook or loon, still, that
don't prove me wrong. Sure, when you look
at it on an individual or personal basis
obviously no one want to make less income.

On the surface a minimum wage seems like a
good thing just like most things that have
create this welfare state beast we have. In
my view even most learned economist
doesn't really understand how a free market
place economy is supposed to work.

The real truth is it is nature's supreme law of
"Natural selection" that really controls
everything in nature including the working of

an economy. And anyone that doesn't
understand nature can never understand an
economy.

The first understanding is listening to the
words, it says natural selection and free
market, force is nowhere to be found. So,
that means the first rule to understanding an
economy is force will never get you the most
production out of an economy.

A minimum wage law is the use of force and
it slows production and may even bring
growth to a halt. Without a minimum wage
law many more businesses could start small
and grow into giants.

Many big business men will tell you that if
they had to start today they could never have
gotten off the ground. All a minimum wage
really does in terms of progress is give more
power to the government to control private
property.

The minimum wage law keeps money inflated
for government to have enough to pay one
group not to work and tax the other group to
death which allows government to stay drunk
on power. Right now the government have

taken over and own far more private property than a hundred years ago and will probably end up owning it all.

Another reason why people don't understand economics is first you have to understand human nature to understand economics. A good example is "Greed," almost everyone thinks greed is a bad thing for an economy, wrong; nothing could be further from the truth.

Nothing can replace greed. There is no greater energy packed motivating force in our entire human makeup than greed. Greed is something that must be harnessed, but, never smothered out or severely restricted if you want a successful economy.

There has never been a rich and prosperous nation without a lot of greedy people to make it happen. Greed can be compared to electricity, very dangerous, but very little progress can be made in terms of wealth without it.

A free market place with free competition is the perfect way to harness greed without smothering or snuffing it out, like the communist or socialist. There never have been and never will be a rich and prosperous pure communist or socialist state.

The USA is no longer even close to having a genuine free market place. A genuine free market economic have never in history failed to produce far more than that nation can use in almost everything.

Yet those in power that love power and control may tolerate the free market but still hate it. The reason power hungry leaders don't like the free market is kin or no kin if you don't produce you are gone.

In closing I will add this little nugget: To create great wealth one must be willing to take great risk. But, no one is going to take great risk without a fair chance for a great reward, period. Why work extra hard and produce more when non producers get an equal share that is where the great USA seems to be headed.

I hope my short economic lecture have been helpful to you in some way. I am a creative self-made writer; most of what you get is my own original thinking.

**SIRMANS LOG: 16 MAY 2013, 2056
HOURS.**

**EXTRA INPUT: 23 MAY 2013, 0135
HOURS.**

Let me say this to around 95 percent of the
USA population that strongly disagrees with
me and my views on abolishing the minimum
wage law, there is a very important question
that you have failed to ask.

That question is: what are you and the
country going to do when the USA
government doesn't have the money and
can't borrow it to pay its bills. Huh! That's the
problem! Over 95 percent of the USA
population have never imagined let alone
asked a question of the sort.

Almost everyone seems to think of the USA
government as some kind of omnipotent
money sow that we can suck on her tits
forever. But, nothing could be further from
the truth. There never has been and never
will be a government that doesn't go broke at
some point.

USA Economy Will Collapse In 2015 Unless 1938 Minimum Wage Law Is Repealed

Even worse, the USA has a social and family provider government that amounts to a socialist welfare state. The USA economy not only can collapse it will collapse as soon as Obamacare fully kicks in in a few months.

No matter what the learned economist and egg heads may tell you, self-made writer little ole me is telling you the USA economy is on the brink and when Obamacare fully kicks in it will collapse.

Sure, probably no one is going to believe me, no problem, we all will know in a few months if the USA economy can swallow Obamacare and survive.

Of course, any suspense could be avoided if the USA just took the bull by the horns and abolished the minimum wage law which would no doubt save the USA economy.

THE "NEW DEAL" CURSE!
Family discipline is the extremely important ingredient that has been missing in the USA ever since the "New deal" seized the provider role from the nuclear and extended family system.

USA Economy Will Collapse In 2015 Unless 1938 Minimum Wage Law Is Repealed

The nuclear and extended family system is where the provider role stayed for over 6,000 years until the "New deal" seized it in the name of Mr. Do-gooder.

However, being a provider is much, much more than just providing food and shelter. The provider is the only one with the power and control to enforce and maintain discipline and instill it in the young.

For any society to survive over four generations the provider must safeguard norms and traditions and make sure they are instilled in the young.

So, when the shallow minded liberals armed with the "New deal" seized the provider role for itself it failed to take on provider duties and responsibilities that have been carried out for over 6,000 years. And the liberals are still doing this crime against USA society.

This shallow senseless liberal destruction has devastated and all but destroyed the African American community in the USA and the cancer is well on it's way to destroying all of USA society.

USA Economy Will Collapse In 2015 Unless 1938 Minimum Wage Law Is Repealed

Now, here we are in the year of our Lord two thousand thirteenth year with 95 percent of the USA population left with the survival instinct of a 10 year old.

We are at death door in terms of human survival with all of our eggs in one basket. We solely depend on a bloated wobbly kneed socialist welfare state beast that could totally collapse any moment and send civilization all the way back to the stone age.

No society can survive without a strong nuclear and extended family system, a strong moral and spiritual code in place, and adequate emergency backup bartering capacity with many small farmers and home gardeners.

Those were the survival tools that allowed western civilization to survive the great depression, which today is practically nonexistent. The stone age may be our only destination.

That is because nature's law of "Boom and Bust" is like the life and death cycle there can be no long term survival unless it is carried out. Yet, here I am with an almost super

natural strong survival instinct and I'm seen
as a nut, kook, loon, or some other reject or
hater.

I plead and I plead for sanity like abolishing
the minimum wage law which I know will
save my beloved homeland, the only home I
know.

Having this great wisdom and super strong
survival instinct is like a curse to me; I can
dissect an economy and see straight to the
core of most things when so many just don't
get it. God, I ask in your name bless the USA
home of the brave and the free.

SLAVE FIELD-HAND MENTALITY GRIP STILL BINDING.

Wake up African American political and
spiritual leadership, grow up and take
responsibility, you are not a field-hand
anymore. You are now up on the hill in the
big house now.

You must now take on the responsibility of
running the place. You must now create your
own jobs and means of making a living. You
must set a budget and make sure the family

gets fed, whereas as a field-hand all you had to do was work and obey orders.

You are now the master of your own destiny now, if you don't do it yourself it may not get done, you are not a dependent anymore. Fast forward to the year of our Lord 2013, the African American race has a serious problem.

People are afraid of African American men, especially young black males. Reality is reality and it is what it is. There is an old saying: You can't make other people change, but, you can change yourself then the world around you will change.

If you don't believe that here is an example: Stress: If anyone on your job or anywhere causes you a lot of stress, just repeat this quote to yourself over and over as long as necessary, "I can wish all people goodwill no matter how they treat me," then the stress will vanish. This is only a tool and not for every situation.

Black males are stereotyped as dangerous and violent prone. A stereotype can be overcome and gotten rid of. You get rid of a stereotype by proving over time that it is no longer true. But, that can't be done until one accepts responsibility and stop blaming circumstance and the system.

There is no excuse why Africans Americans can't obey the law and behave as good as any race, period. Any winning coach will tell you, you are going to get some bad calls but you focus even harder on your game plan.

Sure, as a minority the system may not give a black man a break and in some cases may even be unfair, still, there is no excuse why African Americans can't obey the law and behave as good as any Race.

I'm over seventy and from the Deep South and I remember before the welfare state destroyed the black family, no one feared a black man walking into a country store.

Many years ago in the USA the Japanese were stereotyped as the junk and trinket merchants. But, through hard work and quality control they proved that they could produce as good a product as any nation. Today no one doubts the quality of Japanese products.

USA Economy Will Collapse In 2015 Unless 1938 Minimum Wage Law Is Repealed

African American political and spiritual leaders need to believe and prove that the African American race can behave and obey the law as good as any race, period. Like me or hate me, still, how can any self-respecting responsible African American disagree with me on this, (SMH) shake my head.

The black community itself suffers more than anyone from all of this violence. Do-for-myself responsible hands need to grab the MLK, Jr. baton and take it into the home stretch to full equality and justice.

And, tell the liberals we don't need your pity or patronizing services any longer
SIRMANS LOG: 27 AUGUSTA 2013, 2135 HOURS

IS MASS STARVATION AND SUFFERING AHEAD FOR THE USA?
Almost everyone thinks that I'm really the nut and stupid one for constantly wanting to eliminate the minimum wage law entirely.

Well, I know and anyone with a deep understanding of economics knows that the USA and world economy may soon collapse. When this happens the minimum wage law

will disappear and there may be chaos, mass
suffering, and starvation if we survive at all.

So, all I'm saying is why go through all of
that un-necessarily
when voluntarily abolishing the minimum
wage law will prevent it. One way or another
the minimum wage will go the way of the
great Auk, (SMDH) shake my damn head.

Obamacare is simply the straw that is going
to break the camels back.
**SIRMANS LOG: 25 AUGUST 2013, 1834
HOURS**

"OUR FALSE GOD OF DOOM!"
Just like the big enemy armored divisions of
World War II ran on ball bearings our liberal
created welfare state runs on the minimum
wage law. In sheer economic terms the
minimum wage law is "Our false God of
doom."

It is impossible to save the USA or western
civilization unless the minimum wage law
death grip is broken. The laws of economics
demands that the minimum wage law must
go or the USA bites the dust.

**SIRMANS LOG: 24 AUGUST 2013, 0625
HOURS**

YOUNG CHILDHOOD SEXUAL ABUSE!
This doesn't belong here and I shouldn't be
saying it anyway, it concerns childhood
sexual abuse. My view is very simple; if you
do the crime you do the time or pay with
your life, period.

The good book says flee from temptation,
which a wise man will heed to. Contrary to
what most people may think there are
abnormal forces out there that are almost
impossible to resist unless one flees.

Example: A young child sexually abused may
become obsessed with sex and become
armed with the power of sexual projection.
The child grows up but the abnormal power
of projection remains. Now, if someone with
this abnormal power focuses it on you for
whatever reason, your best bet is to get the
hell out of Dodge and fast.

Enough said, something like this is never
talked about anyway. Ignorance is bliss and
just thank God nothing like this has ever

happened to you. Believe it or not there are forces out there that only a strong moral and spiritual person can withstand, it's rare, but, it does exist.

"The human mind is a very powerful thing".
SIRMANS LOG: 20 AUGUST 2013, 1138 HOURS

IS A GOVERNMENT SHUTDOWN INEVITABLE?

Right or wrong the republicans are stupid if they force any issue that will end in a government shut down. It will be a lose, lose situation for republicans any way you look at it.

The liberals including the vast majority of the mass media in my view will have a blaming field day. Besides, after the first huge public outcry the vast majority of the republicans will head for the tall grass or high tail it out of Dodge anyway. And even if the republicans could win some kind of hollow victory, very little would change, we still remain a welfare state.

This welfare state is on automatic pilot and

nothing or nobody is going to stop it unless its fuel is cut off. Sure, a collapse will stop it but no sane reasonable person wants that, cutting spending won't stop it that will only get the republicans out of office.

Believe it or not, the fuel that propels this whole welfare state is the minimum wage. It is impossible for the USA to survive as a welfare state. But, it is also impossible for the USA to get out of being a welfare state when government sets any wage or price control.

You can't have a true free market economy when government sets any amount of wage or price control. The minimum wage law allows government to inflate the currency so it can keep its power as a super social and family provider.

But, government should never be a social and family provider in the first place because that destroys the nuclear and extended family system. Without a strong nuclear family system it is impossible to remain a free people after four generations.

If the republicans really want to go to the mat for something do something sane like

abolishing the minimum wage law entirely.
That is the only thing that can save our great
nation. yeah! I know! I stand alone on
knowing this fact.

SIRMANS LOG: 4 AUGUST 2013, 2210 HOURS

A Freddie L. Sirmans quote:

Abolishing the minimum wage law will drain
the swamp. The swamp is where the welfare
state beast lives. The swamp is where all of
the anti-survival morality snatchers are
coming from. The anti-survival morality
snatchers are slowly taking over all of our
souls.

TRIVIA NOTE:

Holiday Street in Valdosta, GA. is located
within a few yards of where the home was
located of the famous western gun fighter
"Doc Holiday." It was where he lived as a
teenager before going to dental school and
heading out west.

WISDOM NOTE:

No one can achieve the great supernatural
wisdom that I have without paying an
awesome price to survive, and in my case it

has been a knockout drag out mentally battle
to survive practically all of my life. Still, I
have no monopoly on pain or struggle.

PASSING THOUGHT:

If abolishing the minimum wage law is not
going to be taken seriously by the USA I'm
beginning to suspect the Mayan calendar may
not be very far off the mark after all.

FOREWORDS:

Economic ignorance galore abounds, that's
what it is: This caller made a profound
statement on TV this morning, his view was
that the tax payers were the source of all
government funding. Wow! This guy was on
to something and he knew more than most,
but, he was wrong. Okay, let's do a walk
through.

Government funding does come from the tax
payers, but, where do the tax payers get
their money? All tax payers get their money
from their employers or some type of
business transaction, period. It goes further;
still we haven't arrived at the source of all
government funding.

The real source is what gives in my view the

shallow minded liberals a problem and is the reason liberals with total power is so dangerous to freedom and democracy. The true answer is: All government funding comes from some type of private business profit.

It is all about profit, profit, and more profit and that can come only from private enterprise. The government can only tax profit or the result of some type of profit, otherwise it cannot survive, period.

In general the shallow minded liberals hate the word profit and too a lesser degree hate business people. The welfare state is the reason the man or woman on the street has no concept of the true role of profit except personally having cash in hand.

You can't get blood out of a turnip and government can't tax where no profit is made. Look at Detroit and California all bastions of liberalism. Unless the minimum wage law is abolished to break the liberal death choke hold on the throat of America that will be the picture of the whole country. God save America!

USA Economy Will Collapse In 2015 Unless 1938 Minimum Wage Law Is Repealed

Liberals are who they are and they love America as much as I do even if I do think they are shallow. It is not entirely the liberals fault, it is the system that got us in our dire situation and only the system can save us, that is why the minimum wage law must be abolished entirely.

Everyone wants to make more money and no one want to make less when we can't make ends meet as it is. But, my great supernatural wisdom know abolishing the minimum wage law is the only way out for the USA to survive, period.

If not for the minimum wage law the cost of living for the poor and everyone would drop so they could pay their own food and doctor bills especially with nuclear family help. But, then the government would lose its God like power as a super provider.

The minimum wage law is blocking everything we buy from dropping down where the poor can pay out of pocket like a free market has always worked before the "New deal." It is the buying power of money that truly matters, not some inflated worthless high number.

**SIRMANS LOG: 24 JUNE 2013, 1123
HOURS**

**USA CRIMINAL JUSTICE SYSTEM IS NOT
PERFECT BUT STILL THE WORLDS BEST.**
Let me try to shine some light on this. In the
USA we have an adversarial criminal justice
system which is not perfect but overall still
the fairest known to man.

The prosecutor tries everything it can to win
the case and on the other hand the Defense
tries everything it can to prevent losing the
case. Well. Most of the time somewhere in
the middle justice will be realized but not
always.

The system is not about emotions, right or
wrong, or feelings because then justice would
always be one-sided and never balanced.
However, Joe six-pack and most laymen's
believe that if you commit the first wrong and
a tragedy result the blame is on you, period.

Sure, Christianity allows mercy and
forgiveness, but, when you set a tragedy in
motion you can't expect a pat on the back
and hero worshiping unless racial bias is

involved.

The biggest loser in this whole thing could end up being the Democratic Party. That is because if the blacks stay pissed-off enough they may stay home during the mid term election next year.

This is a dire survival situation in the eyes of most blacks; yet, I for one believe there is some un-necessary stoking of this highly emotional matter. Cooler and calmer heads is what's needed, instead of a lot of flamboyant rhetoric that fans the flames.

SIRMANS LOG: Updated 17 JULY 2013, 1103 HOURS.

OK:
I have commented on this tragedy, so I might as well go whole hog and say what I really feel about the overall African American situation. But, this is an emotional charged issue and I know that truth and reasoning's won't win me a popularity contest.

Sure, there is racialism in America, always has been and always will be. However, racialism may be an obstacle but that is not what is holding African Americans back or down, especially in this day and time. Before the welfare state came along African Americans faced slavery and a far harsher climate than today, Yet, still owned far more.

I'm going to cut right through the chase and strike right at the heart of the African American community problem. I think as a rule African Americans still has a slavery dependency mentality and don't feel entirely responsible for their own survival as a race.

African Americans are stereotyped as violent prone, criminal prone, likely to lower property values, and bring social baggage in most cases. Whoa, anybody thinking that must be a racialist, maybe or maybe not.

What is never said or admitted is every stereotype has a truth foundation. And you can't dismiss a stereotype by ignoring it and making excuses for bad behavior. When bad behavior is excused and ignored it will reflect on the entire race. And it is not facing reality to think otherwise.

Yet, ignoring that fact is typical liberal behavior. By the African American leadership

not taking responsibility for our own behavior
as a race causes us all to suffer the
consequences of being stereotyped in a bad
way. Jealousy, envy, sibling rivalry, and a
host of negative emotions come along with
having a dependent mentality.

Whereas one with an independent mentality
tends to soars above the negative stuff, and
will accept total responsibility for himself, his
race, and his country. As to jobs, the white
man is expected to supply all of the jobs.
There are plenty of African Americans with
plenty of money, why shouldn't blacks as
race be expected to supply more of their own
jobs to their community.

I could go on and on but I think I made my
point; we need to get a grip and feel totally
responsible. I don't have the answer but I do
know before the welfare state no one feared
black men. Before you can solve a problem
you first must admit you have a problem.

I say the African American community has a
problem facing up to the truth. And I think it
boils down to taking total responsibility for
one's own survival. The surest way to cure
dependency is to have the props and crutches

taken away, but that can't happen as long as
we have a welfare state.

Denying truth is the same as denying reality.
And that is exactly what African Americans
leadership and spiritual leaders have been
doing for years concerning black crime. I
have no power to stop bad behavior or crime,
but, you can bet your bottom dollar that I will
never condone it or make excuses for it no
matter who does it.

Folks, I have no power to change anything,
I'm just thankful I can still write and say
what I believe. God Bless America.
**SIRMANS LOG: 19 JULY 2013, 2234
HOURS**

**IT IS NO LONGER A MATTER OF THE USA
ECONOMY COLLAPSING, IT IS NOW WHO
IS GOING TO OWN US**
I keep harping on this evil 1938 socialist
minimum wage law that almost everyone
thinks is a good thing. And again I will repeat
I am one hundred percent dead sure that
repealing this law is the only thing that can
save the USA from total doom.

USA Economy Will Collapse In 2015 Unless 1938 Minimum Wage Law Is Repealed

I am at my wits end, where is our survival instinct as a nation, It's sheer madness the true state of the USA economy, yet we march on like zombies. Never before in history has a civilization allowed it nuclear family structure, culture, and moral values to be almost totally destroyed like what has happen with western civilization.

Western civilization has allowed liberal thinking to flim flam its citizens into thinking the welfare state will always be there to take care of everyone from cradle to grave. Yet, liberals hate profit and have never understood profit which is the engine of economic survival.

Anyone that doesn't understand the role profit plays in a healthy economy is living in fantasy land and can't be trusted in my view. So, when I tell you the evil 1938 socialist minimum wage law is evil you had better believe it.

This nation's sheer survival depends on if and how we get rid of the evil 1938 socialist minimum wage law, period. Power and economics on an individual basis or as nation goes hand in hand.

USA Economy Will Collapse In 2015 Unless 1938 Minimum Wage Law Is Repealed

The true evil of the 1938 socialist minimum wage law is it took the real power away from the economy and the people and gave government almost absolute power. When government can demand what a business must pay it workers no matter how small the economy can no longer protect itself or the nation's inner fabric.

If not for the evil 1938 socialist minimum wage law liberal propaganda could never have wielded the power through big government to destroy our nuclear family system, our culture, and our moral and spiritual values.

With no minimum wage law the USA economy would have had the disciplining power to fight off inflation and big government reckless spending; now USA currency is inflated out of sight.

The evil 1938 socialist minimum wage law must go so the USA economy will again be "Free at last, free at last" to save our nation. Otherwise, it is no longer a matter of the USA economy collapsing, it is now a matter of who is going to own us.

USA Economy Will Collapse In 2015 Unless 1938 Minimum Wage Law Is Repealed

Folks, I am just a lonely self-made writer, I writer what I think and believe. Sure, some of my views are far fetched; still even a broken clock is right twice a day, think about it.

SIRMANS LOG: 25 AUGUST 2014, 1824 HOURS

BEFORE THE "NEW DEAL" THERE WAS NEVER A THREAT TO USA CULTURE, MORALS, AND VALUES!
A lot of people think the USA has always struggled with socialist and others wanting to change or destroy our system of government, and they are right, but there is a big difference in what happening today.

The big difference today is our culture, morals, and values are shot all to hell. With a jury in court or voters in an election no one can truly predict how stupid the outcome may turn out.

before the "New deal" the country went through all kinds of problems and threats but there was never a deadly threat to our culture, morals, and values. Believe it or not, the old saying that no country can afford guns and butter is really true.

That is why Western Europe has already chosen butter, and the USA is now headed that way at warp speed by gutting our military. The destruction of the inner fabric of the USA started when the government seized the social and family provider role for itself during the "New deal."

That was the first dagger stab to our culture, morals, and values. No form of government can survive very long by taking from produces and giving to non produces, in time the load just becomes too great.

The second deadly and fatal dagger stab to our culture, morals, and values was the enacting of the evil 1938 socialist "Minimum wage" law.

That was the coup de grace because a true genuine free floating free market place economy not only safeguards and protects itself; it protects a free nations culture, morals, and values, too.

By enacting an evil 1938 socialist minimum

USA Economy Will Collapse In 2015 Unless 1938 Minimum Wage Law Is Repealed

wage law that crippled and took away the economy's power to discipline itself or the nation. That left the USA with a P. . . . of an economy with no power to discipline itself or fight off inflation.

That allowed the government to inflate our currency and grow government like never before. Sure, all of this government financial power boomed the economy and made masses of people happy, but, was it really worth the total destruction of the nations culture, morals, and values. I personally don't think so, but I'm just one lonely neurotic two finger pecking self-made writer.

I will sum this article up by saying the only thing on earth that has a fighting chance of saving the USA from total destruction is repealing the evil 1938 socialist minimum wage law. And even then it will only give us a fighting chance to overcome four generations of liberal clap trap.

Anyone that doesn't think that norms and traditions matter; need to take a look at religions that have mandatory chants or prayers. That is their secret to remaining unchanged over thousands of years. And they

won't ever change or deteriorate as long they
keep the same norms and traditions going.
Yet, we wonder what happen to the good old
USA? Duh!

Wise men/women has always known that
how you raise your young is not everything,
it is the only thing in terms of long time
survival, period.
Get a grip America. How can you expect the
young to show self-restraint and act
responsible when they have never been
conditioned to show restraint and act
responsible. Duh.
**SIRMANS LOG: 06 AUGUST 2014, 1728
HOURS**

**THE ECONOMY: FIGURES DON'T LIE,
BUT, LIARS SHOW CAN FIGURE!**
Folks, as an extreme and neurotic self-made
writer I don't expect most people to
understand my views. To the shallow I may
seem negative or maybe even a cold hearted
uncaring hater, but nothing could be farther
from the truth.

In fact I believe I am sort of a savior in terms
of helping this great nation survive the

USA Economy Will Collapse In 2015 Unless 1938 Minimum Wage Law Is Repealed

coming troubled times. My view on all of this great news involving the USA economy: Hog wash, hog wash, and more hog wash.

I heard a guy on the radio say that the USA government is a parasite and when a parasite grows larger than it's host it kills it's host. I totally agree with the above statement, the USA government haven't got there yet, but is awful close. Our welfare state beast is fast destroying our job producing free enterprise economic engine.

Every day the USA government grows larger as our profit driven job producing business host sector dwindles smaller. Never mind what the learned economist and egg heads tell you, I'm telling you it is impossible for the USA economy to overall improve or be saved unless the evil 1938 socialist minimum wage law is repealed entirely.

Man alone can't save a dying economy, the same as a doctor alone can't save a dying patient, but a true free floating free market place economy can and will save itself along with it's host nation if unshackled and set free.

USA Economy Will Collapse In 2015 Unless 1938 Minimum Wage Law Is Repealed

Our evil socialist 1938 minimum wage law ties up and restricts our free market place economy to the point where it can't discipline and save itself. And I'm here to tell you I don't care how much tweaking and fine tuning they do nothing can save the USA economy unless it is set free of the evil socialist 1938 socialist minimum wage law entirely.

Good economy news: pure poppy cock, liberals always make things better before an important election, I suspect the cost of fuel will soon be coming down considerably. We all are doomed unless? You know what? We are losing our great USA and it impossible to be saved unless we do what must be done, there is no other way, period.

SIRMANS LOG: 31 JULY 2014, 1821 HOURS

WRITERS VIEW ON THE LAW.
The legislative branch makes the law. The judicial branch interprets and enforces the law according to the constitution. The executive branch carries out the law as is as signed under oath, period.

Now, what the hell should it matter what's
one political view is when it come to the laws.
The law means exactly what it says in plain
English not some subjective liberal hog
wash.

What goes around comes around, and what's
up today may be down tomorrow. Freedom
can't survive with no respect for the law,
period.
**SIRMANS LOG: 23 JULY 2014, 0255
HOURS**

**CONSERVATIVES AND REPUBLICANS
FACE A TERRIBLE DILEMMA!**
The shallow minded liberals over the years
has lied and connived to set the USA on a
course to sure doom. In their minds the end
justifies the means. And they are too shallow
and lack the survival instinct to even know
the damage they have done.

Most liberals see no threat or danger in
spending and want to increase spending and
borrowing to grow government even larger. It
is beyond me how anyone can believe you
can borrow and spend to no end, but liberals

do, I shake my damn head.

They don't see a spending problem with this country at all and if allowed to will spend this great country out of existence, and blame it all on the republicans. My God! What a situation. So you can see, expecting liberals to be responsible and safeguard this nation is a lost cause.

On the other hand, conservatives have an even bigger problem. Conservatives can't seriously plead the case of, "Ignorance is bliss." Conservatives has the capacity and depth to see our great country is on a sure path to disaster.

Conservatives know we are spending ourselves out of existence but face a terrible dilemma on how to stop it. In my view far too many conservatives still want to do the normal right thing of cutting spending and reducing the size of government, wrong. If conservatives do that, they will politically cut their own throats.

USA Economy Will Collapse In 2015 Unless 1938 Minimum Wage Law Is Repealed

Right now that is the worst thing conservatives can do, simply because the liberals has made almost the whole country government dependent to some degree. So, the smartest thing conservatives can do is hold their fire and bide their time before cutting anything.

Talking about controlling spending may work, but to talk about cutting spending and government in this dependent minded climate will definitely keep conservatives out of power.

This writer's position even if no one else agrees with me is conservatives should make it their goal to repeal the evil 1938 socialist minimum wage law. But, never attempt that unless there is a very good chance of success.

Getting rid of the evil 1938 socialist minimum wage law is the only chance of saving the USA from total liberal doom. It shouldn't be planed or talked about just get the power, get in there and do it.

However, there is a big problem, the conservatives disagrees with my views just as much as the liberals.

SIRMANS LOG: 17 JULY 2014, 1605 HOURS

WRITER FREDDIE L SIRMANS SR. DIDN'T WANT TO, BUT JUST HAD TO VENT.
The system can only take so much before it breaks and if that happens we all are in trouble, rich, poor and everyone. I think right now if there is mass disorder our welfare state beast is going for an all out power grab.

The citizen's still has the vote at the present, but, if chaos takes place we may loose that to never regain it. So, when I fill my destiny and keep sending out the stress call to repeal the evil 1938 socialist minimum wage law entirely somebody better listen.

The only thing that can save the USA and individual freedom is a genuine pure free floating free market place economy, period.

USA Economy Will Collapse In 2015 Unless 1938 Minimum Wage Law Is Repealed

And the 1938 socialist minimum wage law is the only thing that is blocking that from happening.

The minimum wage law must be repealed or found unconstitutional or we won't survive the coming doom. I promise you I have the supernatural wisdom and survival instinct to know what I'm talking about.

Nothing and I mean nothing is going to save the USA from a total collapse and doom unless the minimum wage law is gotten rid of one way or another. If you don't believe me just keep on living, we'll all soon find out. We all see our system being put to the test; it can only take so much before something snap.

The thing about a true free float free market place is it doesn't choose sides and has never failed to produce an over abundance of whatever is needed. Who you know or who is under the desk doesn't count if you don't produce.

I don't care if you are liberal, conservative, democrat, republican, or whatever, if we don't get this evil 1938 socialist minimum

wage law repealed or found unconstitutional
we all are going to perish. You disagree,
great; we'll soon see who is right.

I know the general public will never
understand getting rid of the minimum wage
law entirely and I understand that, who
wouldn't won't to make and take home more
money, I know I do. That is why the very
wise founding father made the USA a republic
(If we can keep it).

But, what's at stake here is the survival of
our country and way of life, and I repeat,
there is no way under the sun the USA and
individual freedom will survive with the evil
1938 socialist minimum wage law still in
place, period.

**SIRMANS LOG: 16 JULY 2014, 1639
HOURS**

**GREAT WRITER BREAKS HIS PEN AND
WEEPS!**

Folks, I seem to be some kind of freak of
nature or the victim of some kind of cruel
joke. I am blessed with all of this
supernatural wisdom, but no one listens.

USA Economy Will Collapse In 2015 Unless 1938 Minimum Wage Law Is Repealed

I'm jumping up and down, turning flips, screaming and hollering that the evil 1938 socialist minimum wage law must be repealed entirely or found unconstitutional if the USA is to survive.

Its just that simple, our minimum wage law won't allow for a free floating all powerful free market place economy which would discipline itself and the country, too.

Now, our socialist just like in Western Europe is gutting our military to grow bigger government. The U.S. military is the last uncorrupted great institution left in America, and it can't be rebuilt overnight.

In my eyes the future seems so dim. There is no doubt in my great mind, only a true free floating free market place economy can provide the necessary discipline to save the USA. All that is necessary is to get rid of the choking evil 1938 socialist minimum wage law, otherwise there is no hope.

To be earnest, deep down in my soul I don't think the minimum wage law will ever be repealed. Too few has the wisdom or the survival instinct to see past their noses now-

USA Economy Will Collapse In 2015 Unless 1938 Minimum Wage Law Is Repealed

a-days. I break my pen and weep.

Only the strong survives. The USA is weak in spirit and is the reason we are being invaded. God save the USA.

There is nothing hard or complicated about solving the illegal children invasion problem. The answer is something I have been drum beating on for several years. Maybe there is a divine element about this whole thing.

After all, more people visit a house of worship here in the USA than anywhere in the industrialized world, maybe we are worth saving. The answer to the problem is very simple; just repeal our evil 1938 socialist minimum wage law.

I know, I know, that don't make any sense, where is the connection. You can't see a connection, that is because not everyone has supernatural wisdom and can dissect an economy like this writer can. I'm telling you this type of problem can be unsolvable and may bring the USA to its knee.

You may not agree with the method that I advised, but just remember you have been advised how to solve this problem.

**SIRMANS LOG: 12 JULY 2014, 1008
HOURS**

**FOAMING MAD WRITER RANTS ON, OR,
MAYBE HE IS RIGHT?**

I, great writer Freddie L. Sirmans Sr. rants
on, or, is my super natural wisdom the gospel
truth on what will save America. What most
people fail to understand is that any way of
life will be destroyed in 4-5 generations
unless the proper norms and traditions are
taught to the young.

During the New deal the government seized
the social and family provider role for itself,
and from that time since the poor has
become totally corrupted. Never in history
have the poor murdered unborn babies in the
womb, that was always done by the rich and
well to do.

The poor has always needed children for
labor and to be taken care of in old age. The
poor black man was kicked out of the home
and that left no one to teach and enforce
norms and traditions in the black family unit.

USA Economy Will Collapse In 2015 Unless 1938 Minimum Wage Law Is Repealed

That is why we have all of the insane killing in the black community, that is why there is out of control violence and disorder in the African American community. And it ain't going to get any better until government is out of the social and family provider business, period. Sure, do gooders will talk, talk it to death, but, will never accept a remedy with any teeth in it.

Since the New deal this whole country is not the same country as before. The mentality is not the same anymore. Gone are the old fashion norms and traditions of depending on ones self. The welfare state has long sent any independent frontier like spirit packing.

Hell, almost half of the country thinks the government owes them a living. It's insane, like the USA government can't ever go broke; where in the hell did stupid thinking like that come from. Not only can the USA and world economy go broke, the USA is already there. The USA is living on borrowed time.

The USA doesn't have a pot to piss in. The USA is almost $18,000,000,000,000,000,000 in debt and counting. Due to our welfare state taking away the need for a strong nuclear and extended family system we have nothing to survive on if we can't borrow anymore, its sheer madness.

There never has and never will be a society or nation that survived without a dependable nuclear family system in place, period. Ours are in ruins. Our moral and spiritual values also are in ruins. Today's norm is murdering unborn babies in the womb on demand. And damn the future, just marry the same sex and ignore the fact that there is no future without procreation, who you love is more important than future survival.

What the hell is my problem, I must be mad or some kind of nut talking all of this normal stuff that was the norm 100 years ago. Your kind is not welcome in the year of our lord two thousand fourteen, go back to the twentieth century.

If the economy crashed tomorrow we have practically no emergency backup bartering capacity to buy time on. Call me a nut, kook or whatever, but, I know I am right on my grave concerns. I beg and I plead, repeal the evil 1938 socialist Minimum wage law now, it is the USA only hope of survival on what's headed our way.

Call me stupid or whatever you like but you ignore my concerns at your own risk. Sometimes, I wonder, Is Washington an imaginary metropolis with a lot of kids behind the wheel.

SIRMANS LOG: 10 JULY 2014, 1732 HOURS

IS THE END NEAR FOR A FREE USA
When the USA is 17,000,000,000,000,000,000 in debt and going a trillion or more deeper each year, you are not going to convince me we have a great future or even a future at all. The USA is almost totally at the mercy of its lenders.

If nothing else, at least repealing the evil 1938 socialist minimum wage law would give us a genuine true free market place economy and that would assure our survival under all conditions.

Wake up America and get a tight grip on reality because this nation is fixing to have a very, very rude awakening. Liberalism, liberalism, liberalism, I shake my head.

These illegal immigrant people think they are coming to the USA promise land, so, what went wrong, who are to blame. As a writer, I don't know, but, I suspect the hidden hand is the Dems and liberalism.

Love, caring, and having a sense of compassion are good things and is the spice of life. Life would hardly be worth living without these things. However, these predominate feminine emotions make some problems practically unsolvable.

Most of us know what it is like dealing with a wayward family member. Being an enabler almost never helps. When everything else fails most families just let nature take it course. The same applies to the USA as a nation.

If the minimum wage law was repealed a true free market place economy would kick in and solve the immigration problem, our jobless problem, our social problems, and on and on.

In the end this immigration thing will boil down to a test of the USA character and survivability, will we pass the test? Not unless the evil 1938 socialist minimum wage law is repealed entirely.

I hope I'm wrong. Almost no one agrees with me on this, still, I stand by my prediction. This whole thing is bigger than Immigration alone, it will determine if the USA survives with individual freedom still intact.

Two primary things have allowed the shallow minded liberals to strike at the heart of our system of government and unless that is corrected there is no way possible for the USA to survive as a free nation.

Number one, by enacting the evil 1938 socialist minimum wage law it gave the USA a p . . . . of an economy with no power to discipline itself. Number two, by government seizing the social and family provider role for itself and not enforcing any rules or conditions, that left no one enforcing discipline and passing on norms and traditions for future generations.

A society can't just start over from scratch with each generation and expect to survive very long. The USA is falling apart from lack of sound judgment and character with fewer and fewer people with any common sense.

For example, the law. You don't obey the law because you like it, you obey the law because it is the law. The law is the only thing that protects us all, and especially the poor and powerless. The news media ought to be up in arms with the way the law is flaunted in our faces in high places.

It is impossible for this great nation to remain a free people with no respect for the law like what is happening in the USA today. I rest my case, the jury is still out, we'll see.

No one is above the law doesn't seem to apply anymore in the USA. The bill of rights and individual freedom is something almost unheard of in history before the USA came along, and I use to wonder why.

Now, after seeing what liberalism has done to the USA I understand why freedom is so hard to acquire and hang on to? I just chalk it up as nature knows best. Everything about nature and survival is geared toward struggle.

It is so easy and tempting to just take the course of least resistance and jump on the liberal pie in the sky band wagon. But, I have sense enough to know that no nation can survive without a strong nuclear and extended family system, strong moral and spiritual values, and adequate emergency bartering capacity.

For 6,000 years until the liberal's new deal, governments had the sense to leave the social and family provider role in the hands of the nuclear family unit. Instead during the new deal the USA government removed the need for a strong nuclear and extended family system by seizing that power for itself.

Now, when this whole global economy comes crashing down there is no foundation left to prevent the USA from regressing all the way back to the Stone Age. To me this is common sense thinking, what's wrong with me for wanting to help save my country and survive, shame on me.

Government forcing a evil 1938 socialist minimum wage or price control on a private profit driven business is unconstitutional, period. Of course every worker would be a fool if he/she didn't want to take home more money.

But, force destroys a genuine true free market place economy and results in what's happening in the USA today with no jobs and galloping out of control cost of living. And the really sad part is it's only the tip of the iceberg before total collapse and doom.

SIRMANS LOG: 03 JULY 2014, 1908 HOURS

IS ILLEGAL PROSTITUTION SHUTTING OFF A SOCIETAL RELIEF VALVE?
The subject of prostitution is where you will find more hypocrites and self-righteousness than anywhere else. I'm not condoning anything, I'm just writing my views and

observations. When you go back in history
one thing all civilizations had in common was
they had the wisdom to leave certain things
alone. Prostitution was one of those things.

It has always been legal and tolerated
throughout history for a very good reason.
But now, especially many of the hypocrites in
the USA and western Europe think it is the
devils workshop. And what do we have,
untold numbers of perverts, child molesters,
and sex offenders all because the little head
took over in a moment of weakness. Why
shouldn't there be a legal means for these
men to find some relief?

In fact, in my view it is shallow and stupid to
make prostitution illegal, why do you think
we have so many child molesters and all
kinds of perverts? Sure, regulate it and keep
it under control but it should never be made
illegal. Mother Nature gave great pleasure to
eating and sex to make sure there will be
future generations. Therefore, those with real
wisdom tend to leave prostitution alone as a
necessary sin and not preach and fool around
with it.

Prostitution is a venting mechanism that

takes pressure off the good decent nuclear family way of life. There are certain things we can pretend to get rid of, but in reality we can't and still remain civilized. We may be human, civilized, and all that, but we still have animal instincts. Right now, there is more sneaking around after dark than most of us would like to believe. Sexual energy is no fantasy it is physical and real whether we like it or not.

It is one of the most powerful forces in our entire make up. Sexual energy will build up like pressure in a steel drum and if it is not vented in a harmless way society is going to pay a price. It's not something that can be snuffed out without serious side effects; sages of the distance past understood that. Just look around to where the force of some of this energy is popping out in perverted ways. There is a reason why the world's oldest profession is still around.

Many will strongly disagree with my observations on this, but in my view the oldest profession has always been and will always be a societal relief valve. It is a relief valve for the unmarried and many other situations. Common sense should tell you what happens when a relief valve is closed off, something is gonna blow. Men by nature are aggressive creatures and sometimes one slight touch or one show of affection will prevent total self-destruction.

As it is those that are ugly, antisocial, and with many other imperfections can't find legal sexual relief. Most men can channel their sexual energy into other productive things, but some cannot. Why do you think we have such a long list of child molesters and other perverts now days? My guess is un-vented sexual energy is one leading cause. With no legal relief of sexual energy the only choice for many is manual self-relief (with the aid of porn).

To get sexual relief a lot of men have sold out their soul and true beliefs, then start believing their sold out views as fact, that is one reason why you see so many spineless men today. Most of us have seen cases where a young man stays in trouble and is out of control, and then he finds a girl friend or gets married and becomes as calm as a cucumber. Sure, he may feel more responsible, but the main reason is most of his aggression is being vented.

USA Economy Will Collapse In 2015 Unless 1938 Minimum Wage Law Is Repealed

Capitalizing on self-sexual relief is what's behind and driving this whole out of control invasive video pornography sex industry. There may be a lot of lookers, but the ones actually spending big money and buying are viewing for masturbating purpose, which is supporting and allowing all of this sluttish invasive stuff to be in our face. Why would one pay to watch a video when they can legal get the real thing.

Sure, a few might but I don't believe the big bucks would be driving porn like what is happening now. Surprisingly, women make up almost half of these buying consumers (which may include a bathroom ceremony complete with candles).

Come on folks! Far too many men are watching porn, and what woman ain't got a hidden toy, give me a break, who knows, maybe it's just me imagining too many things, maybe I should admit publishing this whole article was a gross mistake and pretend it never happened. Forgive my bad judgment folks, lesson learned.

However, I got news for anyone watching too

much pornography. It can dull ones sexual
imagination and lock one into a visual
stimulation only mode in order to stay
aroused. And make even a teenager addictive
to where normal sex is not possible. My
intent is not to write how thing should or
should not be, but to write things the way
they really are.

This is more wide spread than you may think,
many young men after a night of partying
prefer to cap the night home alone
masturbating to porn. My god! If that ain't a
threat to the future I don't know what is. So,
"How do you like me now?

SOMETHING ABOUT THE WRITER:
I, Freddie Lee Sirmans, Sr. was born during
the war years in a little Georgia town off
Highway U.S. 129 not far
from the North Florida border. It was in the
winter of `42, three days before
Christmas, Dec. 22, 1942, in Stockton,
Georgia. I was the forth of seven surviving
children in a group of fourteen. Unfortunately
seven of those children died before I
was born. My early years were spent playing
and enjoying life.

I remember vividly a little lake right beside

USA Economy Will Collapse In 2015 Unless 1938 Minimum Wage Law Is Repealed

Highway U.S. 84 that we used to play in
as young kids. None of us could swim. We
used to call it the clay hole. At the time I
guess I was about ten or eleven years old.
We didn't have any swimming trunks so
we would all swim naked. The water was sort
of dark, but we all felt safe once we
were in the lake. The challenge was to watch
for cars passing on the road or anybody
walking by.

The regular gang included my brothers Buie
C. and Bernard "Rip", my cousin J.E.
Burgess, neighboring kids Spencer Bines and
sometimes Bo Bo Brown and I. My
older brother Marvin Elder and a few other
older neighboring boys, Joe Louis
Glover, Ellis Williams, Johnny Lee "Sweet
Pee" Dorsey were much too mature for
our group. I can't remember if my younger
brother, Jimmy, four years younger than
I, would ever come along.

We would take off all of our clothes, hide in
the nearby bushes, and as soon as the
coast was clear we would run and dive into
the lake. The deepest spot was not over
three and a half feet. And one of our biggest
fears was that some grownup would
come down to the lake and stay, because we
would be ashamed to come out of the
lake naked. I can't remember who the lady
was, but I remember she walked down
from New Prospect Baptist Church about a

quarter of a mile down the road.

She walked right to the edge of the lake and
started chewing us all out. I guess she
had some kind of insight into our fears and
shames, because she would not leave; she
was determined to wait us out. We were all
cornered and ashamed to come out of the
lake. So after what seemed like an hour, it
was getting late in the evening. Lady or
no lady, we decided to make a run for the
bushes where our clothes were hidden.

Everyone was embarrassed, but we knew we
couldn't stay in the lake till dark. My
father was a domineering, unyielding type of
individual. One of my first experiences
with his unyielding stance was my bed-
wetting. I was a bed-wetter until I was
approximately six or seven years old. My
father's way of dealing with bed-wetters
was an automatic whipping, with no
exceptions.

That's just the way it was. No matter how
hard I tried, I could not stop wetting the
bed. I kept getting older and kept getting
whippings, and the gladdest day in my life
was when I quit wetting the bed. That meant
I would not be getting whipped almost
every morning over something I could not
avoid. It left emotional scars that are still
with me to this day. It saddled me with a
pitiful look that I hated, and caused me to

harbor a secret inferiority complex all through childhood.

It left me with a neurotic pitiful look that would at times take over my brain like an epileptic seizure especially if I was very tired or stood before a large crowd of strangers. I have come a very long ways in mentally overcoming this handicap mostly through the positive thinking technique.

However, you never erase anything from the all powerful mind, all anyone can do with a handicap is face it down and learn to forgive and accept it, then you will survive. My battles with self-shame has been a lone internal war but I have no regrets; it has made me a better human being with an almost super mind in some ways. I thank you God for my life, health, and strength.

I felt I could not let anyone get too close because something was wrong with me, and if people saw how pitiful I could look they would reject me, laugh at me, or feel sorry for me. Each reaction was unacceptable. I just wanted to be normal and accepted, no more or no less. I guess I was around nine or ten when my family moved about four miles to my grandmother's farm.

There again I felt the effects of a completely

domineering and unyielding father. My
father didn't give any warning like, "Don't do
that again." As a young aggressive
kid, I was expected to act good, but I was
branded a bad boy and I guess I acted the
part, because over a two year span, it
seemed like I would get a whipping almost
every day for something or other. Then all of
a sudden it stopped.

I guess my spirit was broken. To me it didn't
seem like I was doing anything
differently. All I knew was I was glad I was
not getting whipped almost every day.
All of my young life was not miserable, in fact
overall I was a very happy kid. Then
and now I never held anything against my
dad or took it personally. Sure, my dad
may have been somewhat too strict, but we
are all human and no one is perfect, I can
earnestly say that overall I knew him to be a
good and decent man.

I thank God he taught us seven kids how to
survive with pride and dignity. Not a one
of us has ever spent time in jail, and we are
all over fifty. We all work to earn our
keep, and we don't want or expect handouts
from the government or anybody. It was
mainly a matter of ignorance. My father
raised me like his father raised him, and his
father before him. Besides, the older I get the
more I appreciate a strict raising, but
not one without love.

USA Economy Will Collapse In 2015 Unless 1938 Minimum Wage Law Is Repealed

If I had to choose between a raising of over-permissiveness or over strictness, I
would choose the latter. It assures the best chance of survival under all conditions,
but a balance between the two is always the most productive. I'd never be too hard
on misfortunes, because they may save one from a more disastrous or fatal end. Just
remember the Lord works in mysterious ways.

Sometime when one is rushing to get some place and nothing seems to work right,
who knows that delay may have saved one from a fatal accident. Life is all about
timing. Maybe not all, but some of us have a destiny, and must be prepared for the
mission. I feel it is something bigger than an individual; even bigger than life itself.
Like an idea whose time has come, it can't be held back, but so long, it has to happen.

In spite of my handicaps I have long known my mission and destiny must be
something almost out of this world big, just maybe, it may be to help save western
civilization in a recognizable way, little ole me. Praise be to God.

In 1955 they closed the two-classroom school house in Stockton, Ga., and I attended
the seventh grade over in Lakeland, Ga., the county seat. We sharecropped the farm

one more year with Isben Livingston that my
grandmother's heirs had sold him the
year before. Then in the summer of `56, the
Charlie Sirmans' family moved from
Stockton, Ga. to Valdosta, Ga.. There my
father became a taxi driver. Mother dear,
Alberta, a lovely, non-complaining, passive
woman was in frail health.

She had suffered the first of her many
strokes. I attended the segregated Pinevale
High School. I excelled in basketball and
football. I was a member of the Pinevale
Tigers basketball team. I can still cock my
head and imagine hearing the basketball
cheerleaders chanting, "Freddie! Freddie!
Freddie! He's our man, if he can't do it
nobody can." I finished high school in 1961
and turned down a basketball scholarship
to attend Fort Valley State College in Georgia.

It was the alma mater of my late high school
basketball and football coach, Edward
Jones of Quitman, Ga. He believed in me and
thought very highly of me. I will
always remember how he walked to my
house in the rain to bring me the news of my
basketball scholarship. The only other
member on the basketball team to get a
scholarship that year was Oswell Jones, who
went into the U.S. Army.

I later went into the U.S. Air Force. I worked
a while at South Ga. Pecan factory in

Valdosta, Ga., and then about the middle of
1962 I decided to move to Tallahassee,
Florida, to attend a trade school. The name of
the school was Consolidated
Electronics. I went to the school about two
hours a day, and got a job in a little
delicatessen and donut shop on Adams Street
near the old capitol building.

I rented a room from a lady named Mrs. Ford
who lived right in front of the funeral
home on Carolina St. I stayed there for about
six months until the school ended.
After returning to Valdosta in late 1962, I
decided to enlist in the U.S. Air Force.
Being a young man, I spent some of my
leisure time cruising North 24th Street in
Omaha, Nebraska. At that time there were
two nightclubs we used to hang out in,
the M&M Lounge and the Off Beat Lounge.

Then I moved on to Puerto Rico for my last
two years in the military. While there, I
bought an old 1952 Studebaker. I still have
fond memories of the Caribbean and the
tropical climate. Still young and enjoying life
sometimes we would check out Isabella,
but mostly we would hang out in the little
coastal town named Aguadilla. At that time
In Aguadilla they had a night club called the
Black Stallion where most of the airmen
hung-out.

I distinctly remember they had one famous

patron called Casa Boo Boo (house
ghost). She was as black as the ace of spades
and very ugly, but she must have made
up for it in other ways because she always
got her share of dates. In 1966, after four
years in the U.S. Air Force I got out and
returned to Valdosta. I had turned down my
basketball scholarship, so my goal was to get
a college education.

At that time they had a four year, fully paid
GI Bill that would pay you while you
attended school. Then I missed my ship
again. I got a job, got married and started a
family. I don't regret anything. Now more
than twenty five years later, and over age
fifty, I feel maybe I have something
worthwhile to say. I wrote a few letters to
the
editor that gave me some courage. Now here
I am after writing four books and
reprinting my first book.

I'm no intellectual; I am a high school
graduate with one semester of college while
in
service. But I have done a fair amount of
reading along the way. My writing should
be raw, crude, and pure, so hang on for a
ride.

YEAR 2011 ADD-ON:
First, let me take this time to count my
blessings. Lord I have so much to be

thankful
for, I have a great family that loves me
dearly. Thank you God, thank you, thank
you
for my life health and strength. This once
beaten down pitiful little South Georgia
USA country boy has kept the faith and is still
standing. "May the life I have lived
and the works I have done speak for me,"
thank you God, thank you.

On this day in the year of our Lord Twenty
Eleven A.D. Saturday the first day of
October, I, Freddie Lee Sirmans Senior again
just took time to count my blessings.
Three days before this Christmas I will
celebrate my sixty ninth birthday December
22, 2011. However, still the effects of my
childhood bed wetting punishment days at
times haunt me. There are no doubt the
mental scars and effects will go with me to
my grave.

I, so much like everyone want to be proud
and stand proud, but for me sometimes it
is still a great struggle, the helplessness
neurotic pitiful look still tugs at my soul. To
me it is all about survival, I accept no
excuses or blames for survival because I
believe if you are looking you can always find
an excuse for failure. I have fought
mental battles to survive practical all of my
life, and will never surrender. It is said
that behind every super achiever there is a

search for love and acceptance, I believe
that.

"To try and keep trying is the greatest of all
virtues. Winners don't quit and quitters
don't win." Think you for taking the time to
read about me, with love always,
Freddie L. Sirmans, Sr.

****

****

Version #2 Has additional information.
I was born in the early forties in a quiet little
Georgia town near the Florida border.
It is located at the intersection of U.S.
Highway 84 east to west and U.S. Highway
129 north to south. I was delivered by a
midwife three days before Christmas,
December 22, 1942 in Stockton, Georgia. I
was somewhat puny and was not
expected to live. I was the eleventh child in a
group that would eventually reach
fourteen children.

Unfortunately seven of those fourteen
children died before I was born. I was a very
sensitive kid, always snotty nosed, but I
survived. The old frame house that we lived
in was like many houses built around the turn
of the century. The kitchen was
separated from the living quarters of the
main house. In our house, in order to get to

the kitchen, you had to go outside and walk
down a long porch to reach the kitchen.

We didn't have electric lights, and I
remember at night someone older had to
carry a
kerosene lamp down that seemingly long,
long porch, and I would be so afraid. One
of my earliest memories in that old house
was that I would get a whipping almost
every morning for wetting the bed.

It left me with a neurotic pitiful look that
would at times take over my brain like an
epileptic seizure especially if I was very tired
or stood before a large crowd of
strangers. I have come a very long ways in
mentally overcoming this handicap
mostly through the positive thinking
technique.

However, you never erase anything from the
all powerful mind, all anyone can do
with a handicap is face it down and learn to
forgive and accept it, then you will
survive. My battles with self-shame has been
a lone internal war but I have no
regrets; it has made me a better human
being with an almost super mind in some
ways. I thank you God for my life, health,
and strength.

I remember we had a fireplace, and one
morning I was standing with my back to it

warming up. I had on some ragged bib
overalls. All of a sudden I felt something hot
on my leg, and when I looked down, I saw
that my pant's leg was on fire.

I took off like a bat out of hell not thinking to
smother the fire. I could have easily
sustained third degree burns all over my
body or lost my life because I would never
have stopped running. Fortunately, there was
a bed in the room and I ran into it,
thereby allowing enough time for my sister
Betty and brother Buie to reach me and
smother the fire. A large burn mark still
covers most of my left leg today. I hated
short pants.

It seems as if I was fifteen years old before
my mother would let me wear long pants.
Most kids my age were wearing long pants,
and I felt only little kids wore short
pants. I wanted to be mature and grown up,
not a little kid in short pants. Most of my
earlier years were spent playing and going to
the clay hole in the summer. The clay
hole was a little man-made lake right beside
U.S. Highway 84. Also about one
quarter of a mile down the road was New
Prospect Baptist Church.

It was at the church where I had to wear
short pants and say an Easter speech every
Easter. The regular members of the
swimming gang were my brothers Buie and

USA Economy Will Collapse In 2015 Unless 1938 Minimum Wage Law Is Repealed

Bernard (Rip), my cousin J.E. Burgess, the neighbor kid Spencer Bines, sometimes BoBo Brown, and I. My older brother Marvin was much too mature for us. Our house was the old Corbin home. My grandfather Henry Corbin had moved to Waycross to work for the railroad years ago.

I guess I was around nine or ten when the family left the old Corbin home and moved about four miles to my grandmother's farm. It was the Sirmans' home place that my great-grandfather Steve "Buck", a slave, settled on when he became a free man. My grandmother, Alice Roberts Sirmans, who was born about 15 miles away in Mayday, Georgia was half Cherokee Indian and half white.

She had been living at the farm when we moved in but moved shortly thereafter to a house in Valdosta, Georgia that my father Charlie and my uncle Freddie had recently built. There on the farm I was expected to do my share of the work. I remember very clearly that complaining did very little good. I remember we had to pick up sweet potatoes after they had been plowed from under the ground.

You had to stay bent over for long periods of time. I would tell my mom or dad that my back was hurting, and they would say, "Boy! What do you mean your back is

hurting? You don't even have a back at your
age. All you got is gristle." I cropped
tobacco and hung it in the barn, but the most
hated job was gathering corn in beggar
weeds. The corn and the beggar weeds would
cause your skin to sting.

Then around 1954 the Sirmans' heirs got
together and sold 100 acres of our farm
land to Isben Livingston. My dad bought the
other 100 acres of the wood land that
our house was on which he sold a few years
later. In 1955 they closed the two
classroom school house in Stockton, Georgia
and I attended the seventh grade over
in Lakeland, Georgia the county seat. Then in
1956 the Charlie Sirmans' family
moved to Valdosta, Georgia.

My dad became a taxi driver. That year I was
in the eighth grade, and I started the
school year in the old Dasher High School
that had been downgraded to a junior high
school. At that time a strong disciplinarian,
highly moral, and spiritual man, patrolled
the halls. That man was Professor J.L. Lomax,
the principal, whom the school was
later named after. I, like the other students,
was terrified and scared to death of
being caught in the hall unauthorized.

The new school, Pinedale High, had just been
completed. For some reason, I can't
remember exactly why, they had added two

eighth grade classes to the new high
school that first year. Thereafter it was only
grades ninth through twelfth. I was in
one of the two eighth grade classes attending
that first year in 1956. I believe my
home room teacher was Ms. Carrie Lissimore.

The principal, Mr. C.C. Hall, the late band
director, Mr. C.D Marshall, the chorus
and others agreed that the school's new
anthem did not rhyme properly with the
word Pinedale. Everyone agreed that Pinevale
rhymed almost perfectly with the new
anthem, so the school was thereafter known
as Pinevale High. "Good old Pinevale
High we will live and die for you, for you."

I was very insecure and shy in high school
and will probably be somewhat shy and
insecure all my life. I remember very vividly
an incident that happened to me in Ms.
Sarah Jones' class. I guess I was in the
eleventh or twelfth grade. I had my shoes
leaned on their side under my desk, and
when I shifted their position on the tile floor
it sounded just like someone passing gas. All
eyes focused on me, but I never looked
up, I just kept my head hung and bowed.

After what seemed like a slow motion minute,
Ms. Jones casually and quietly walked
over and opened some windows near where I
was sitting. After the class was over a
small lad that sat right next to me, I can't

remember his name, but he walked up and
told me, "I know that was your shoe that
made that noise" and I told him that it truly
was. The reason I mention this incident is
that because of my shyness and insecurity
at the time I failed to set the record straight.

Even if I didn't have the courage to speak up
then, I should have at least went to Ms.
Jones later and set the record straight. But
instead I remained mute, and to this day
as far as I know only that young lad in that
whole class knows that I was innocent.
Unlike most of today's young men, I was a
late bloomer. I had come close, but when I
finished high school I had not had a
consummated relationship. In fact, my first
consummated relationship came around the
age of twenty.

In high school I was a jock. I was crazy about
girls, but I was afraid to go after them.
I excelled in sports, so that became my
primary interest. When I graduated in 1961,
only two members on the basketball team
received scholarships, Oswell Jones and I.
We each received basketball scholarships to
Fort Valley State. We used to call
Oswell the Big "O". To this day I can honestly
say Oswell was one of the best
basketball shooters I have ever seen.

Even in high school if he got hot he could
consistently hit 25 foot jumpers. I am sad to

say that he was a victim in a fatal car
accident while returning to Atlanta from the
"92" Valdosta High School Wildcats State
AAAA Championship football game,
which Valdosta won. I can still remember
one of the chants that the Pinevale High
basketball cheerleaders would yell out.
"Freddie! Freddie! Freddie! He's is our man,
if he can't do it nobody can!"

I finished high school in 1961 and then
worked a while at South Georgia Pecan
Factory in Valdosta before moving on to
Tallahassee, Florida to attend a little trade
school. The name of the trade school was
Consolidated Electronics. I went to the
school about two hours a day. I managed to
get a job in a little bakery and
delicatessen shop on Adams Street right
around the corner from the old capital
building.

I got a room with Mrs. Ford who lived right in
front of a funeral home in French
Town on Carolina Street. I stayed in
Tallahassee for six months until the little
trade
school ended. After I returned to Valdosta in
late 1962, I decided to enlist in the U.S.
Air Force. Like most new recruits in basic
training, I visited the Alamo in San
Antonio. From there I spent two years in
Omaha, Nebraska. At that time, GI's didn't
make as much money as they do today, but

we knew how to party on what we had.

They had a barbecue shack at that time on
North 24th Street. They sold a whole slab
of rib for about $4.95. Today it would cost a
lot more. We would buy a fifth or two of
white port or red port wine for about $2.00 a
fifth, get fired up, then each of us would
get a slab of rib and party into the wee hours.
 But the downside on duty the next
morning I would feel like I had been shot at
and missed but S... at and hit. About five
months before I left Omaha, I met Janet.
That is all I care to say, but she was special
and I will never forget her.

I was young and not very responsible in that
department. Even when young I tended
to talk as a philosopher when someone would
listen, and that she certainly would do.
I would try to figure out her problems and
the why of things. When I left I gave her
my home phone number in Valdosta. When
she called me while I was on leave, I
acted like I didn't want to talk to her. That
was the last I ever heard of her. I don't
know why, but maybe something in my
childhood caused me to feel ill at ease
talking
to the opposite sex in the presence of my
parents.

That is what happened to me when Janet
called. When she called I guess I seemed

like a different person, like I didn't care. But I
really did care. Even today it saddens
me how it ended. When I got out on my own
and got married that type of behavior
didn't occur any more. My last two years in
the military were spent in Puerto Rico. I
bought a 1952 Studebaker and enjoyed the
Caribbean and tropical climate.

I also enjoyed some red beans and rice, the
islands' staple, plus some fresh roasted
pig. The little coastal town of Aquadilla is
where we did most of our partying. The
Air Force no longer has a base in Puerto Rico,
but at that time in Aquadilla there was
a night club called "The Black Stallion" where
most of the airmen hung out. I clearly
remember one famous patron. She was as
black as the ace of spades, and they called
her Casa Boo Boo. She also was very ugly
and had a face only a mother could love.

But she must have made up for it in other
ways because she was never lacking. She
always got her share of dates. My enlistment
was up in September, 1966. I got out of
the military and returned to Valdosta. My
goal was to get a college education. There
was no excuse not to because I had a four
year fully paid GI Bill at that time. I also
would receive pay while going to school. But I
guess it was not to be because I found
a job and a girlfriend. I got married and
started a family.

USA Economy Will Collapse In 2015 Unless 1938 Minimum Wage Law Is Repealed

I do enjoy reading and doing crossword puzzles, two hobbies I think would be good for anyone planning to write a book one day. I grew up with an inferiority complex and was a very insecure person. I still am not out of the woods, but I have made a lot of progress. I have greatly increased my self esteem and learned how to do for myself. Sure, I wanted a college education and could still complete a degree at my present age.

But I decided to sacrifice the prestige and overcompensate in some other area of achievement. I have operated several small businesses over the years, including the Super "S" Restaurant for over a year and a janitorial service for more than fifteen years. Also, this is my second book. The title of my first book was, "The Black Psyche In America". So overall I don't regret anything. My formal education is limited to a high school diploma and two college courses for one semester while in the service.

My writing should be raw, crude and pure, so hang on for a ride. I know everyone can't agree with a lot of what I write, but that is what's so great about this great country. Everyone has the right to express his own beliefs. I have chosen to express some very strong views on social issues. I expect some very strong disagreements. So I wish only one thing to those disagreeing. Please disagree without becoming disagreeable.

I BELIEVE IT'S TIME FOR MEDICAL SUPERVISED FLOGGING TO BE TRIED

I believe societal-wise four or five hard lick on the rear will do more to reduce crime than ten years in modern day prison. That would be especially true with the black young and first time offenders. And the big advantage is its practically free with no housing and caretaking cost to the tax payers.

Flogging is nothing new and it works. There is a lack of real discipline in the early raising in most African Americans homes today. That lack of discipline is a failure to instill self-restraint which makes one aware of consequences. I think it is time the whole USA criminal justice system considers experimenting with flogging seriously.

The prisons nationwide are already filled to the brim. Daily as I listen to the local news there is smash and grab, break-ins, muggings, and crime, crime galore. Hell, I know I'm barking up the wrong tree, because oh no, we are too civilized to stoop to something so primitive as flogging.

I'm just saying we are being over run by

crime and taking care of all these law breakers are just too expensive. I'm not talking about the sadistic cold hearted murders and rapist; of course they must be kept locked away. Folks, I'm a writer and I call a spade a spade and tell it as I see it.

It is not going to get any better folks, either we control crime or it's going to control us. We know it is a fact that young African American males are committing crimes far out of proportion to their population. We also know that African American mothers shapes and molds the character of these young men more than anyone else.

Our culture is so damaged that most Americans will see me as a hater and the bad guy that doesn't care about young black men, wrong. However, the real truth and long tern survival of our nation is I am willing to try to save these young men and our nation, too.

A few whacks on the ass may hurt some feelings and may even break a few heart but it won't kill anyone, whereas to do nothing or lock someone away for 5-10 years is a waste of time and money in my view. Get a grip and wake up America, this welfare state is on its way out.

SIRMANS LOG: 08 MAY 2014, 2239 HOURS

DISTRUSTING BLACKS

Maybe something is wrong with me as a black man because I easily understand cause and effect, which I don't think most African Americans do.

I hear so many rich, famous, and educated African Americans bitching and moaning because taxicabs don't want to stop for African Americans. And why African Americans are stopped so much more by law enforcement and on and on why blacks are picked on.

It is the same as many people saying we live in the richest and most powerful country in the world, yet, doesn't have a clue as to why the USA is the most richest and most powerful country. African American thinking has not always been corrupted like it is.

Before the "New deal" African Americans took pride in working harder and being better at things. Before the new deal almost no one feared and distrusted African Americans in their home, in a store, or anywhere. I live in a small southern town and watch the local news, and almost everyday there is crime, crime, and more crime.

Its smash and grab, breaking and entering, muggings, shootings, killings, and on and on. And it's African Americans who are committing 80-90 percent of all of this crime.

USA Economy Will Collapse In 2015 Unless 1938 Minimum Wage Law Is Repealed

Yet, we have African American leadership and liberals bewildered and can't understand why law enforcement and other races fear and distrust us as a race.

I just don't get it, what am I missing here. To me it is cause and effect as plain as day; I shake my damn head, duh. Sure, all races commits crime, but, my God, not over five times out of proportion to your race population. We as a race are actually doing far, far more crime, so how can we as a race solve the problem if we won't accept that fact without misplaced blame and phony excuses.

Even Immigrant blacks obey the law, so why are so many of my fellow African American so in denial and ignorant of any cause and effect due to breaking the law. I blame it all on the "New deal" destruction of the black nuclear family by kicking the poor black man out of the home, and the enacting of the evil 1938 socialist minimum wage law.

SIRMANS LOG: 20 AUGUST 2014, 2244 HOURS

HEALING QUOTE: "I can wish all people goodwill through God which
strengthens me." One can leave off the through God which
strengthens me or substitute in place of God ones own deity.

USA Economy Will Collapse In 2015 Unless 1938 Minimum Wage Law Is Repealed

Just repeat the quote to yourself as many times as necessary or
until the storm passes over. No one else has to know what you are
repeating to yourself.

I promise you if you have trouble on your job, in your marriage, or
whatever, your stress will vanish, it is not a cure all, but, a stress
free healing process will began.

True joy and happiness comes from within. But, you can't find it
from within. You find it by caring, helping, and serving others!

DIABETES HELPFUL HINTS
Every diabetic should read labels and keep count of the amount of
carbohydrates consumed. Carbohydrates are really what determine ones
blood sugar level. If carbohydrates can be kept down to around 50g per
meal it will go a long ways in controlling ones blood sugar level.

Meats and fats without anything added like sauces and gravies don't
contain carbohydrates. Most leafy vegetables and others like greens
beans, broccoli, cauliflower, and sweet peas average around 15g per 1/2

cup. It is the big 5 that can be enjoyed but really need to be kept under
control, they are bread, rice, potatoes, pasta, and artificial sweets.

My healthy eating priority formula: Eat, fresh and raw when possible,
cooked fresh, cooked frozen, and lastly cooked canned. However, as a
rule eating food properly cooked is always safer in my view. I'm not a
trained medical professional in any way; I'm a self-made writer and hope
my limited knowledge will be helpful to someone in some way.

WRITERS OPINION ON PUTTING ETHANOL IN GASOLINE!

I think putting ethanol in gasoline was one of the cruelest hoaxes ever pulled on the American people. Anyone that have an older or any car that is seldom driven is going to have problems.

With ethanol in it gasoline deteriorates so rapid that the gas tank needs draining after a few months or so if not used. Plus, sooner or later it is going to drive the cost of all corn products out of sight.

I have an old classic car that I seldom drive and I gotta find me some ethanol free gasoline somewhere. Sometime later, shame

on you Freddie Sirmans Sr, for thinking there
is still individual freedom left in the USA to
buy ethanol free gasoline!

Hell, how was I to know that it is mandated
by the Feds that ethanol free gasoline can no
longer be found in this great free country. I
guess I will just have to drain all of the gas
out of my old classic car and keep the tank
empty or run the hell out of it. Wake
up America!

They do have perservatives one can add to
the fuel, but it is still a dumb idea putting a
vegetable product in gasoline.
**SIRMANS LOG: 12 MAY 2010, 0029
HOURS.**

**IS A PERPETUAL MOTION ENGINE
POSSIBLE?**
The idea of a perpetual motion engine has
been around probably as long as engines
been around. Inventors has used compressed
air, battery power, and anything you can
think of trying to keep a engine running
almost forever.

All for naught, the idea is an illusion. But,
there are still people around today that think
it's possible. It is the same way with an
economy. There are still far too many people
around today that think you can forever run
an economy without a rebirth.

USA Economy Will Collapse In 2015 Unless 1938 Minimum Wage Law Is Repealed

The facts are the same, it is all an illusion, and it can't be done. In economic survival terms stocks, bonds, and everything done on Wall Street is an illusion and side issue. No portfolio means anything if money has no value.

And even if money has value it means nothing if you have no food to eat or if those that have food won't sell. As I have said many times in terms of raw survival money are way down the list, people survived long before money was invented. In terms of long time survival culture is far more important than money.

No amount of money can save a nation when everyone is at each others throat. If the USA culture was strong and healthy far more people would agree with me and realize the only way to save the USA is to junk the minimum wage and cut taxes to the bone.

I can only hope I'm wrong, because I believe when we starts starving in mass numbers it will be because no one can start small and grow. It will be because the minimum wage and sky high taxes won't let entrepreneurs feed themselves and the nation.

Rich people are not the same as poor people with money, there is a world of difference in motivation and mentality. Lottery winners have proven that fact. When have any lottery winner ever built a financial empire that employed a hundred thousand people.

Socialism and communism fails because there are no entrepreneurs. And there are no entrepreneurs because there is no extra reward given for extra effort. Everybody tries to give the least amount of effort to survive.

No one in America have ever had to live in a system like that, we all need to be counting our blessings. Sure, everyone will be equal, but equal poor. I say, hell no!

MASS FUEL SAVING VEHICLES AIN'T GONNA HAPPEN IN THE USA!

The technology to produce a vehicle that would cut fuel consumption almost in half has been around ever since the late 1950's. From an economically point of view there are thousands of things made from oil from the pavement we drive on to the clothes on our backs, but fuel consumption is the lions share.

The reason no genuine serious effort to produce a mass fuel saving vehicle is not going to happen is because big business and the government wants more profit and revenue not less. Sure, there is some fiddling around and pretending to make a mass produced fuel saving vehicle but that is just throwing out a bone to fool the public.

If you think I'm wrong about a fuel saving vehicle take a look at the diesel locomotive. Two or three diesel locomotives can pull hundreds of box car all day long without gulping fuel. The reason is they have no drive train. The diesel engine powers a generator that supplies electrical power to electric motors for the wheels. And it's been that way ever since the late 1950's.

Sure, automobiles need quick acceleration for passing but with technology a way could be found to overcome that. All I'm saying is that in the real world what saves or works best don't always win out.

To sum it up, once the "New deal" gave the government an excuse to seize the nuclear family provider role for itself the destruction of the USA economy die was cast, estimated collapse time 4-6 generations into the future. As a super social and family provider the government is going to fight tooth and nails any and every decrease in revenue.

That is why government as a family provider will never allow a free people to remain free for very long. I have been out here screaming and hollering about the dangers of the welfare state to deaf ears now for many years.

But, I believe time is winding down and more and more of my great wisdom is going to be realized and appreciated. I thank you God for my life, health, and strength. I carry on and refuse to stand down America.

I'm at a loss as how to think and act any other way. I give God the Praise, thank you God, thank you, thank you...

THE END

WRITER: Freddie Lee Sirmans, Sr.
Website: www.FLSirmans.com/index